INTENTIONAL HELPING

A Philosophy for Proficient Caring Relationships

John J. Schmidt

East Carolina University

Merrill
Prentice Hall

Upper Saddle River, New Jersey
Columbus, Ohio

Library of Congress Cataloging-in-Publication Data
Schmidt, John J.
    Intentional helping : a philosophy for proficient caring relationships / John J.
Schmidt.
      p.   cm.
    Includes bibliographical references and index.
    ISBN 0-13-085845-5
    1. Helping behavior. 2. Caring.   Title.

   BF637.H4 S37 2002
   158'.3—dc21   2001030322

Vice President and Publisher: Jeffery W. Johnston
Executive Editor: Kevin M. Davis
Associate Editor: Christina M. Kalisch
Editorial Assistant: Amy Hamer
Copyeditor: Dawn Potter
Production Editor: Linda Hillis Bayma
Design Coordinator: Diane C. Lorenzo
Text Designer: Ed Horcharik, Pagination
Cover art: SuperStock
Cover Designer: Thomas Mack
Production Manager: Laura Messerly
Electronic Text Management: Marilyn Wilson Phelps, Karen L. Bretz, Melanie N. Ortega
Illustrations: Erika Quiroz-Heineman
Director of Marketing: Kevin Flanagan
Marketing Manager: Amy June
Marketing Coordinator: Barbara Koontz

This book was set in Garamond ITC by Prentice Hall and was printed and bound by R.R.
Donnelley & Sons Company. The cover was printed by Phoenix Color Corp.

Prentice-Hall International (UK) Limited, *London*
Prentice-Hall of Australia Pty. Limited, *Sydney*
Prentice-Hall Canada, Inc., *Toronto*
Prentice-Hall Hispanoamericana, S. A., *Mexico*
Prentice-Hall of India Private Limited, *New Delhi*
Prentice-Hall of Japan, Inc., *Tokyo*
Prentice-Hall Singapore Pte. Ltd.
Editora Prentice-Hall do Brasil, Ltda., *Rio de Janeiro*

10 9 8 7 6 5 4 3 2 1
ISBN: 0-13-085845-5

To Dawn, Eric, and Evie Bergquist,
whose intentions have filled our lives with joy

About the Author

John J. (Jack) Schmidt is a professor and chair of the Counselor and Adult Education Department at East Carolina University (ECU). Named Distinguished Professor for the ECU School of Education in 1999, he has been a teacher, counselor, school system director of counseling services, state coordinator of school counseling services, and university professor for more than 30 years. Dr. Schmidt is an active writer, having published more than 50 professional articles, chapters, technical manuals, and books, including *A Survival Guide for the Elementary/Middle School Counselor*, *Counseling in Schools* (4th ed.), *Living Intentionally and Making Life Happen*, and *Invitational Counseling*, with William W. Purkey. A recipient of many professional honors and awards, Dr. Schmidt has been active in the counseling profession, holding many state positions, including president of the North Carolina Counseling Association, and serving on the editorial boards of professional journals. He also served several terms on the Board of Licensed Professional Counselors in North Carolina.

Foreword

This book is about purposeful caring in professional helping relationships. *Intentional Helping: A Philosophy for Proficient Caring Relationships* builds on the rich tradition of caring advocated by Arthur Combs, Sidney Jourard, Nel Noddings, Hugh Prather, Carl Rogers, Gilbert Wrenn, and others. It extends this tradition by recognizing the critical importance of intentionality in caring, which involves both purpose and direction.

Until now, intentionality has been largely overlooked by those writing about professional helping. A recent survey of professional counseling texts revealed that very few even indexed the term *intentionality*. This should be a cause for concern, for intentionality is at the heart of professional helping.

As Schmidt explains, intentionality is the filter through which individuals give meaning to the experience of living and thus are able to link their internal dialogue with overt actions and skills. Intentional caring for oneself, others, and the larger community provides a theory and philosophy of practice for helping.

In six succinct chapters, Schmidt explains the anatomy of intentional caring, describes practical ways to create and maintain caring relationships, and provides a series of questions and ideas to encourage the reader's reflections about personal and professional functioning. An unusual and most helpful feature of *Intentional Helping* is its emphasis on balancing skill, knowledge, and care. This balance involves being intentionally helpful with oneself and others both personally and professionally. Overlooking or neglecting one dimension causes stress on others. The secret is to be purposefully inviting in balancing all four dimensions.

Intentional Helping will be a valuable resource and practical guide for counselors, psychologists, social workers, nurses, and allied professionals who wish to benefit from a fresh and innovative perspective of human service. This book is an invitation to care more purposefully and to feel more deeply about people. The ultimate measure of caring, according to Schmidt, is how helpers treat those closest to them. All the professional success in the universe will not make up for lack of success with those we love and who love us.

As Nel Noddings reminded professional helpers, if we desire a more caring society, we must model one. Schmidt's refreshing book provides a beautiful and much-needed model of intentional caring for professional helpers.

William Watson Purkey
University of North Carolina at Greensboro

Preface

Professional helping in the form of counseling, therapy, nursing, social work, and allied fields has moved beyond artful practice into the realm of science and skill. Research and literature now focus on specific skills, short-term therapy, and outcome-based research, thus furthering the development and efficacy of professional helping. At the same time, however, this emphasis on the technology of helping might persuade professionals to ignore the important role of humanistic beliefs and core conditions in the development of successful helping relationships.

Intentional Helping: A Philosophy for Proficient Caring Relationships is a brief treatise about the purposeful integration of caring with appropriate knowledge and skill. It continues the tradition of Carl Rogers (*A Way of Being*, 1980), Milton Mayeroff (*On Caring*, 1971), Rollo May (*Love and Will*, 1969), Eric Fromm (*The Art of Loving*, 1963), William Purkey (*Invitational Counseling*, 1996), and other writers who have promoted the act of caring as requisite to establishing healthy and helpful relationships. As such, this book is a philosophy that can guide counselors, social workers, and other helpers as they use their knowledge and skill for the utmost benefit of people who seek their assistance.

Primarily written for counselors, clinical social workers, therapists, health care providers, and other professional helpers, this book may also be valuable to laypersons who volunteer their time and expertise in helping others. It is intended for students who are planning to enter the helping professions as well as for practitioners who want to reflect on the helping relationships they establish every day with students, clients, and patients. *Intentional Helping* is not a comprehensive text on helping skills or theoretical approaches. Rather, it is a supplementary guide to the theories, skills, and knowledge that proficient helpers bring to every helping relationship. For this reason, the book is a brief presentation intended as a reflective discourse. Readers who want a more in-depth study about particular aspects of helping are encouraged to explore the references cited throughout the book.

Intentional Helping: A Philosophy for Proficient Caring Relationships consists of six chapters. Chapter 1 introduces the concept of caring, contending that it is an essential condition for helping. Three elements of intentional caring are explored:

(1) the importance of knowing what it means to care, (2) knowing oneself, and (3) understanding people who seek assistance.

Chapter 2 introduces the construct of intentionality and illustrates the interaction between a helper's intentions and degree of caring. This chapter highlights the importance of direction and purpose in helping relationships and advocates a balance of care so that both parties within a relationship receive adequate attention while maintaining a broader interest in the welfare of the group, institution, or society. The intentionality of the helper also encompasses the ability to encourage those seeking help, provide appropriate support, and persevere with difficult clients. Sometimes people who seek professional counseling staunchly protect their self-beliefs, although such beliefs risk failure or more tragic outcomes. At these times, an intentional helper's caring takes the form of perseverance and gentle persistence.

Chapter 3 examines the prerequisites and structure of caring. First, it considers an understanding of human perception and how such understanding provides a foundation for caring. Second, it presents the fundamental belief that caring professionals use their knowledge and skill only for beneficial purposes. They understand that therapeutic knowledge and skill include an inherent responsibility to practice ethically—that is, always in the best interest of the individual and with a high respect for the welfare of the total group. Finally, the chapter revisits some of the essential ingredients of caring, including trust, flexibility, and positive regard.

Chapter 4 presents a paradigm for creating beneficial messages within an intentionally caring relationship. Included are the desire to help; the need to be prepared; the conditions for creating, sending, or not sending helpful messages; the value of knowing how to resolve differences; and the importance of measuring the progress of any helping relationship. This chapter ends with practical ideas and strategies to facilitate caring in difficult situations.

Chapter 5 asks helpers to self-reflect by examining how they care for themselves. In addition, this chapter explores how important it is for helpers to tend to their relationships with clients. The belief put forth here is that the counselor, nurse, therapist, or other helper has primary responsibility for ensuring the welfare and safety of those who seek their help. At the same time, helpers must maintain their own emotional, physical, and mental health and accurately reflect on how they contribute to or detract from others' quality of life.

Chapter 6 continues the self-examination begun in Chapter 5 by asking helpers to move beyond individual helping relationships and assess how their work contributes to the well-being of society. How do they seek to belong in positive ways to establish community with others? How do they demonstrate love to the people who are most important in their lives? The ultimate test of caring helpers is how they treat those closest to them.

Throughout each chapter, I offer vignettes called "Reflections" for you to consider when examining your development as an intentional helper. These musings can be used individually to explore your self-understanding or be discussed in seminars and other classes for students entering the helping professions.

ACKNOWLEDGMENTS

Many people have supported and assisted with the development, research, and writing of this book. I am forever grateful to my mentor, friend, and colleague William Purkey for including me in the development of invitational counseling and the numerous writing projects we have published. His instruction and guidance have been extremely valuable in my development as a professional and a person, and I sincerely appreciate the foreword that he wrote for this book.

Thanks also go to Kevin Davis, my editor, who invited me to publish this book even before I put a word on paper. His thoughtful reactions and careful guidance throughout the project were very helpful. I am also indebted to Christina Kalisch, associate editor, whose correspondence and management of the review process were invaluable.

Much of the research for this book was accomplished with the help of Gene Saunders, who was my graduate assistant during the early stage of the project. I am grateful for his excellent work.

The final version of this book is the product, in part, of many excellent reviews received during the writing phase. I thank the following reviewers for their helpful comments and valuable suggestions: Willis E. Bartlett, University of Notre Dame; Linda L. Black, Northern Illinois University; Tom Brian, University of Tulsa; Samuel T. Gladding, Wake Forest University; Bette Katsekas, University of Southern Maine; Merle Keitel, Fordham University; Becky J. Liddle, Auburn University; and Paul W. Power, University of Maryland.

I also want to give special thanks to Marilyn Sheerer, the dean of the School of Education at East Carolina University, and to many colleagues whose support of my work encouraged me to write this book. Lastly, I give my love and appreciation to Pat, my wife, best friend, and partner, without whose patience and support the completion of this and all my publications would not have been possible.

Discover the Companion Website
Accompanying This Book

THE PRENTICE HALL COMPANION WEBSITE: A VIRTUAL LEARNING ENVIRONMENT

Technology is a constantly growing and changing aspect of our field that is creating a need for content and resources. To address this emerging need, Prentice Hall has developed an online learning environment for students and professors alike—Companion Websites—to support our textbooks.

In creating a Companion Website, our goal is to build on and enhance what the textbook already offers. For this reason, the content for each user-friendly website is organized by topic and provides the professor and student with a variety of meaningful resources. Common features of a Companion Website include:

FOR THE PROFESSOR

Every Companion Website integrates **Syllabus Manager**™, an online syllabus creation and management utility.

- **Syllabus Manager**™ provides you, the instructor, with an easy, step-by-step process to create and revise syllabi, with direct links into Companion Website and other online content without having to learn HTML.
- Students may log on to your syllabus during any study session. All they need to know is the web address for the Companion Website and the password you've assigned to your syllabus.
- After you have created a syllabus using **Syllabus Manager**™, students may enter the syllabus for their course section from any point in the Companion Website.

- Clicking on a date, the student is shown the list of activities for the assignment. The activities for each assignment are linked directly to actual content, saving time for students.
- Adding assignments consists of clicking on the desired due date, then filling in the details of the assignment—name of the assignment, instructions, and whether or not it is a one-time or repeating assignment.
- In addition, links to other activities can be created easily. If the activity is online, a URL can be entered in the space provided, and it will be linked automatically in the final syllabus.
- Your completed syllabus is hosted on our servers, allowing convenient updates from any computer on the Internet. Changes you make to your syllabus are immediately available to your students at their next logon.

FOR THE STUDENT

- **Counseling Topics**—17 core counseling topics representing the diversity and scope of today's counseling field
- **Annotated Bibliography**—seminal works and key current works
- **Web Destinations**—significant and up-to-date practitioner and client sites
- **Professional Development**—helpful information regarding professional organizations and codes of ethics
- **Electronic Bluebook**—send homework or essays directly to your instructor's email with this paperless form
- **Message Board**—serves as a virtual bulletin board to post—or respond to—questions or comments to/from a national audience
- **Chat**—real-time chat with anyone who is using the text anywhere in the country—ideal for discussion and study groups, class projects, etc.

To take advantage of these and other resources, please visit the *Intentional Helping: A Philosophy for Proficient Caring Relationships* Companion Website at

www.prenhall.com/schmidt

Contents

3

Anatomy of Intentional Caring   39

4

Creating Caring Messages   55

5

Doing for Oneself What You Expect of Others   75

Beyond the Helping Relationship   91

1

The Heart of Helping

As I care for others and am cared for by them, I become able to care for myself.

Nel Noddings
Caring: A Feminine Approach to Ethics and Moral Education, 1984, p. 49

Helping exists in countless forms and in both professional and volunteer relationships. In all instances, what is fundamentally important includes not only the skills, techniques, or knowledge we bring to the relationship but also the *willingness* we demonstrate to reach out and care about others. This essential ingredient of caring is what initiates a helping relationship and allows it to continue toward a successful conclusion. It is the core—the heart, if you will—of the helping process. Without sincere care about the people we attempt to help, the process might simply become a mechanistic exercise to accomplish an identified task or assist with a problem.

Helping is comprised of involvement, participation, instruction, advisement, and other aspects of relating to individuals or groups of people for the purpose of bringing about meaningful change or making healthful decisions. In professional helping relationships, counselors, nurses, social workers, and others use their knowledge, skills, and techniques to assist students, clients, and patients in solving problems, making decisions, maintaining healthful lifestyles, and reaching other life goals. Career transition, family disruption, surgical recuperation, and educational goal setting are among the variety of issues addressed by a wide range of helping professionals.

As noted, skills, knowledge, and appropriate techniques are important aspects of helping; but without genuine care about the people who seek our assistance, we might not always realize outcomes that contribute to beneficial growth and development. In this book, I present for your consideration a philosophy that says helping relationships based solely on method, technique, knowledge, and skill cannot be consistently and dependably successful. As Combs and Gonzalez (1994) indicated, "effective helping is not a simple question of learning how to teach, counsel, nurse, administer, or whatever" (p. 27). Instead, the incorporation of appropriate knowledge and skill into a personal theory and system of beliefs about the practice and process of helping enables us to be successful with the students, clients, and patients we serve.

In this chapter, we will explore the condition of caring as an essential part of a helper's philosophy. Our purpose is not to diminish the importance of knowledge and skill but to emphasize the *intentional* union of genuine caring with appropriate helping methods and processes. By themselves, knowledge and skill put the helping professions into a category of technicians, methodologists, analysts, and manipulators. While these skilled practitioners provide valuable service in repairing machinery, designing research, and understanding social phenomena, they do not require the deep appreciation of caring within a human context that we expect in intentional helping relationships.

Many of the helping professions have become so sophisticated in their use of methods and techniques that the essence of caring is overlooked. Biofeedback, desensitization, lifestyle disclosure, hypnosis, behavior modification, pharmacology, and a host of other strategies and interventions are available to counselors, social workers, therapists, and health care professionals—and most, when applied appropriately, do help people create a better quality of life. Still, these are simply tools that practitioners use; and without genuine concern and regard for patients and clients, they might not enable us to establish truly helpful relations.

This book encourages a balance in how we perceive the role that caring plays in all our helping relationships. It returns us to some of the basic premises put forth by earlier proponents, including Arthur Combs (1989), Sidney Jourard (1964), Rollo May (1969), Milton Mayeroff (1971), C. H. Patterson (1959), Carl Rogers (1951), and C. Gilbert Wrenn (1973). At the same time, it promotes a fresh examination of caring qualities encouraged by contemporary authors such as Nel Noddings (1984, 1992), Alfie Kohn (1991), and William Purkey (Purkey & Schmidt, 1996).

The characteristics of successful helping relationships are interdependent. Therefore, caring and other human conditions are intertwined with our skill and knowledge, enabling us to forge a beneficial direction and worthwhile purpose in our helping relationships. Of all these aspects, caring is most important because it gives every relationship positive direction and a humane purpose. Without this element of caring, we might establish relationships with direction and purpose that are less than effective with those whom we intend to help.

Sometimes helpers might be so intent on the method or procedure they are using that they lose focus on their primary purpose. For example, a school counselor trying to help a student win new friends might be so interested in teaching assertive skills that caring about the student's goals becomes secondary to the learning objectives set by the counselor. Other times, we observe working relationships that are less than helpful because a counselor, nurse, or other practitioner is more concerned about institutional policies and administrative guidelines than about the welfare of his or her clients. Such behaviors violate the true meaning of helping because they lack the fundamental attribute of caring—what Rogers (1980) referred to as "unconditional positive regard" (p. 116). When we allow ourselves to be manipulated by organizational circumstances or become so entrenched in our own agenda, we risk losing sight of the essence of helping relationships. At these moments, it might be helpful to reconsider the fundamental meaning of caring.

WHAT IT MEANS TO CARE

We demonstrate caring for others by the countless ways that we show regard and concern toward our fellow human beings and the world in which we live. As noted, helpers have the skills and knowledge to assist people. The philosophy put forth here claims that without proper care, however, their skill and knowledge may be insufficient and at times even counterproductive. Furthermore, helpers who genuinely care proactively seek out people and situations that need attention. Caring helpers rarely sit back and wait for people to ask for their assistance.

Every day we find examples of helpers who reach out and care for others. Often these acts are simple gestures that go almost unnoticed by those whom they intend to help. For example, opening a door for someone, picking up a stray piece of paper in a public hallway, cleaning off our table at a fast-food restaurant, and passing by a parking space so another driver can have it are ways to show kindness and courtesy toward others. When we act in this manner on a consistent basis, showing routine acts of kindness, we demonstrate higher levels of caring.

Sometimes we hear about or witness powerful demonstrations of human caring, generosity, and kindness. These acts are unmatched by any caring behaviors we have seen or could imagine doing ourselves. Strangers who stop at disastrous accidents and without hesitation risk their lives to save others exemplify this level of caring. Professional fire fighters, rescue workers, and police officers who go beyond reasonable expectation to save lives, protect people, and serve the community also offer us countless examples of caring at the highest level of functioning. In all these commonplace and extraordinary illustrations of caring, we may wonder what motivates people to extend themselves and reach out to others.

Our desire to care for and about others is stimulated in a number of ways. Wuthnow (1991) offered five reasons for caring, the first of which is a natural impulse to

Reflection

Think of a time in your life when someone helped you. Recall this event in as much detail as you can, remembering specifically what the person did that was so helpful and your feelings as the situation unfolded. What do you remember about the event, and what lessons do you believe you have incorporated into your philosophy of helping?

help others. For some people, the innate emotions linking us to the human experience are so strong that we respond naturally to people and situations that call for assistance. As mentioned, we often observe this natural impulse during tragic accidents, when some people are moved to immediate action while others stand by and watch. Professional helpers and volunteers demonstrate this impulse to care by going above and beyond the expectation of their role. For example, a physical therapist who listens with compassion to clients' concerns while performing needed treatment conveys a willingness to connect in ways beyond the basic client-therapist relationship.

A second motivational factor in caring is the utilitarian purpose that often underlies caring behaviors. Many helpers operate from a belief that their actions should be directed toward providing the most benefit to the largest number of people. Such utilitarianism is exemplified when people are available to help on any occasion and in all situations. They continually seek ways to make the world a better place for everyone to live.

Volunteerism is a third factor in caring. Volunteers have many reasons for reaching out to others and donating their time for particular causes, and among them is the primary motivation to give back to the community. Serving on fire and rescue squads, helping out in homeless shelters and soup kitchens, picking up trash in "adopt a highway" programs, and tutoring students in schools are just a few examples of how people volunteer. At various times, volunteerism reaches a high point in our communities. For example, during certain holidays emphasizing spiritual renewal, people discover a motivation to help in ways that may not be apparent during the rest of the year. Among Christians, we witness this phenomenon during the Christmas season, when social agencies often turn away volunteers because the sheer number is too great to handle. Religious tradition is another factor that stimulates caring behavior.

Lastly, we desire to care for others because the action is self-fulfilling. When we give part of ourselves to help another person, our lives are enriched and our self-concepts enhanced. This process relates to what Rogers (1961) referred to as our tendency to actualize ourselves. Thus, by genuinely caring for others we create a direction in our life that expresses our unique selves and our potential for growth. By contrast, people who are inhibited in caring about others or, worse, are destructive in their relationships have lost this tendency to self-actualize due to psychological distortions and disturbances.

All these motivational factors are considered when we examine the role of caring in our helping relationships. Certainly, the natural impulse to care has had some role in leading to our career choice in the helping professions. People do not choose counseling, nursing, social work, or similar professions unless they have some inclination to work with people and help make lives more productive, healthy, and fulfilling. By the same token, helping professionals and volunteers want to have a beneficial purpose that moves beyond the individual toward an impact on the larger community. For example, school counselors help students achieve academically in hope that their efforts will contribute to a knowledgeable and productive citizenry.

Likewise, social workers assist families with financial aid that contributes to the economic stability of the community. Their efforts to help individual families may have expanded benefits such as lowering the crime rate and decreasing incidents of domestic violence.

Volunteerism, spiritual inclination, and a drive to seek self-fulfillment give additional meaning to our caring efforts. Professional helpers often go beyond their defined roles, voluntarily providing additional assistance when needed. For example, a college counselor who walks a new student across campus to locate a service moves beyond the counselor-client relationship to being a practical and voluntary caring helper. It would be easy and convenient for the counselor to give the student directions: "Turn left out the back door, go past the fountain on the square, enter the red brick building on your right, and go to Room 210." By taking time to walk with the student, however, the counselor lends personal attention to a seemingly mundane task. Sometimes these simple gestures we give freely are the strongest demonstration of caring.

Strong religious beliefs or spiritual guidance, which sometimes elicits caring behavior, often influence helpers. In certain helping professions, such as counseling, we are cautious not to let our religious beliefs unduly influence practices. To do otherwise may be unethical according to professional codes. Lastly, self-fulfillment is a motivator because, as an outcome of helping, it energizes us to enter new relationships with enhanced confidence that we can provide assistance and be a beneficial presence in the lives of other people. When we are successful in our helping relationships, we feel good about the contribution we have made in assisting another person or other people.

EMPATHY AND CARING

For professional helpers, empathy plays a key role in establishing and maintaining successful relationships. It is an essential aspect of counseling, psychotherapy, and other helping relationships. Sometimes in describing these relationships, we mistakenly use the terms *empathy* and *caring* interchangeably. Although each is important, both have distinct meanings. By definition, *caring* is the process of demonstrating concern, attention, and an inclination to help or protect someone. As we have noted in this chapter, it is a process that consists of different factors and, when incorporated into a professional function such as counseling or nursing, includes many attributes and qualities.

Reflection

Recall a time when you helped someone. What factors influenced your willingness to help in this situation?

Empathy is a particular quality that we sometimes find in caring relationships. We define it as the quality of appreciating and understanding the perceptions of others in a way that enables us to enter their world of feeling and thinking. When we behave in empathic ways, we demonstrate "an accurate . . . understanding of the client's world as seen from the inside" (Rogers, 1961, p. 284). By demonstrating this accurate understanding, we form a unique and subjective relationship with our clients. Such an intimate relationship not only challenges our clients to assess their perspectives but might also encourage us to rethink our views about life. For this reason, we take a degree of personal and professional risk when achieving empathic understanding in any of our relationships.

According to Patterson and Hidore (1997), empathic understanding is different from scientific understanding that results from external references. In their view, empathy emanates from an internal perspective. Therefore, in the context of empathic understanding, counselors, psychotherapists, and other professional helpers are not as concerned with learning particular facts about their clients as with understanding clients' perceptions and feelings about themselves and their inner world.

As part of the caring process, we convey empathy by listening fully to clients, attempting to understand their viewpoint, and responding appropriately to show we comprehend. As empathic helpers, we accept what people tell us. This does not necessarily mean agreement on our part, but we listen and receive these messages without judging or introducing our own preconceived ideas. Through accurate listening, by seeking clarification of clients' statements, and by trying to see issues through the eyes of our clients, we come as close as possible to understanding their feelings and thoughts. Lastly, we communicate our understanding clearly to clients, who subsequently might increase their faith in us as caring helpers. This cycle of empathic listening, understanding, and communicating allows the relationship to progress toward a deeper and more meaningful level of helping.

Rogers's (1980) summary of the research on empathy in therapeutic relations has value today and can be applied to our definition of the caring process. An adaptation of his summary highlights some of these conclusions to help us understand the relationship between being a caring person and being an empathic helper:

- *A caring helper is, first of all, empathic.* The key to helping is our understanding of the client's or patient's point of view.
- *A correlation exists between our empathic understanding and the progress we make in helping relationships.* Research indicates that empathy correlates with a client's willingness to self-explore in therapy. Empathy demonstrated early in the helping relationship is predictive of a successful outcome.
- *A caring helper empathizes freely with all clients.* Speculation that empathic helpers might be influenced by the types of clients (i.e., appealing or attractive) that they serve has not been supported by research. If an empathic climate exists, we can assume that a caring helper has created it.

- *Empathy is a special ingredient in all helping relationships, and professional caring offers more of it than do friendships or similar relationships.* This finding supports the notion that our professional skill and knowledge, when used appropriately, play a vital role in demonstrating empathy within all our helping relationships.
- *Our clients and patients are the best judges of the degree to which we empathize as helpers.* A parallel finding is that helpers are not as accurate in judging their own level of empathy. This means that counselors, therapists, and other practitioners must rely heavily on the perceptions of their clients about the quality of the helping relationship.
- *Empathic understanding can be learned from empathic people.* Perhaps one of the most powerful outcomes of caring relationships is that the people involved learn to care for themselves and others more than they did previously. The finding that empathy can be learned by being with empathic people may provide one of the most important reasons for caring helpers to practice with empathic understanding. Cultivating systems of care is a purpose of helping that we will consider more fully in Chapter 6.

ASPECTS OF CARING

Caring as a process consists of many factors and qualities. Mayeroff (1971) enumerated the qualities of caring as knowing, alternating rhythms, demonstrating patience, being honest and trustworthy, showing humility, having hope, and maintaining courage. Each plays a significant role in the helping process. As helpers, we incorporate these and other qualities into every relationship, and the degree that we are able to demonstrate these characteristics of care is proportionate to our success as helpers.

Knowledge is a critical aspect of all helping relationships, although this may seem contrary to common beliefs. Sometimes we might think that knowledge is not essential in caring for others—that simply caring is enough. Although this may be true on occasion, in most ongoing helping relationships we must offer more than good intentions and positive regard.

In professional helping relationships, knowledge plays a role in both our general understanding of the situation and the specific skills, information, or other expertise we contribute to the process. For example, a nurse in an emergency room has broad understanding of nursing practices, hospital procedures, and emergency routines. In addition, nurses have general understanding of patient care, communication, and unique differences that patients bring to every medical relationship. At the same time, an emergency room nurse is skilled to respond appropriately to a range of critical and life-threatening conditions, each of which has its own specific requirements. The nurse uses technical skills and medical knowledge that are essential to each emergency situation. Combined, this general knowledge and these specific skills enable the nurse to care for people; and by being successful with individual patients, the nurse increases general knowledge of nursing practice. In Chapter 2, we will explore further the importance of knowing in a caring relationship—specifically, the idea of knowing what to do and why to do it.

The use of alternating rhythms (Mayeroff, 1971) mirrors the idea of being flexible and spontaneous in helping relationships. Professional helpers sometimes repeatedly use the same gesture, intervention, or strategy regardless of its effectiveness. A counselor, for example, who always applies the same type of intervention without thought or regard for the client's perceptions may be locked into a particular rhythm of helping, a pattern that might not be very effective with a wide range of clients. Likewise, a therapist who unwittingly repeats the same phrase, "Really? Tell me more," regardless of what has been said, illustrates an unintentional mode that devalues the client's perspective. When we lock ourselves into one course of action for every situation, we neglect the client's or patient's perspectives. Even when we are successful with these strategies (meaning that a particular goal is reached), we may be so focused on doing one thing that the broader helping relationship suffers. Such a posture diminishes the possibility of establishing truly caring relationships.

In contrast, when we alternate rhythms, we choose our responses, interventions, and strategies carefully and demonstrate a willingness to vary behaviors based on the situation at hand and needs of those who seek our assistance. By doing so, we expand our platform for caring and resist the temptation to become locked in a single mode of operation. Truly caring professionals maintain a flexible stance that permits choice and spontaneity within a responsible framework of practice. Sometimes this might mean acting on our instincts rather than relying on some set formula that we have learned in our professional or volunteer preparation. Analogously, Dass and Gorman (1985) wrote, "Our impulses to care for one another often seem instinctive. The more we're able to act on them freely, the more opportunity we have to feel whole and helpful" (p. 11).

The mind sometimes restricts our helping relationships. On the one hand, our mental monitoring is important to ensure responsible practice. On the other, it sometimes limits what we choose to do, thereby inhibiting the care we ultimately intend to give. In a sense, this is a struggle between our heart and mind. The heart wants to care in the most flexible and open way, but the mind sets limits to maintain the integrity of the helping process. Perhaps by alternating rhythms, we are better able to keep appropriate balance so that the heart behaves in a responsible manner while the mind searches for ways to expand our limitations.

On occasion, helping relationships do not progress as smoothly or quickly as we would like. Perhaps the client is resisting change or the patient is not consistently following prescribed instructions. Maybe there is an external factor inhibiting progress. Whatever the reason, these delays and barriers sometimes try our patience and threaten our ability to care. Patience is another important aspect of caring, one that is closely related to unconditional positive regard (Rogers, 1951).

Patience in caring relationships permits us to give time to the process of helping. Such time is valuable to us as helpers and also to our clients and patients. We use time afforded by our own patience to assess where we are in the relationship and evaluate our own development as professional caregivers. In the teaching profession, this approach is known as *reflective practice*, meaning that we think about what we have done or what we are doing in the process of teaching others. Such reflection takes time. Similarly, our patience allows clients the time to process information, make choices, and assess their own development within each helping relationship.

Mayeroff (1971) offered two descriptors that explain how patience contributes to caring relationships: tolerance and growth. By being patient with our clients, we allow ourselves and them to grow and develop in a reasonable span of time and in a way of their choosing. The counseling profession suggests that tolerance of ambiguity is an important characteristic of successful counselors (Wiggins & Weslander, 1979). Perhaps in other helping professions, the tolerance of clients' confusion and floundering is also important. Being tolerant of people's unique characteristics—for example, their cultural heritage—is essential to all caring relationships. Through such tolerance we demonstrate patience and give clients time and space to develop in ways that enrich their lives, and ours as well.

Honesty and trust are two aspects of caring that we will address throughout this book. On the surface, they are easy concepts to understand, but in practice both retain a complexity that can lead to misguided and mistaken behaviors. As Mayeroff (1971), Rogers (1980), and others have noted, honest relationships are founded on more than a principle of what not to do. In other words, our honesty with students, patients, and clients is based on more than simply not telling untruths or lies. At the same time, caring relationships exhibit honesty with high respect and sincere regard for everyone concerned. For this reason, we are careful about our frankness with clients and avoid being brutally honest when the occasion calls for caution in how to convey important or delicate information.

Through helping relationships, we learn that being genuine with clients is the way to demonstrate our honesty and trustfulness. What we say is reflected in what we do with our clients. At the same time, there is congruence between our feelings toward clients and their issues and our actions in helping them deal with concerns. This depth of honesty is what Rogers (1980) referred to as *realness* in the helping relationship, an essential element in all significant relationships: "Congruence, or genuineness, involves letting the other person know 'where you are' emotionally. It may involve confrontation and the straightforward expression of personally owned feelings—both negative and positive. Thus, congruence is a basis for living together in a climate of realness" (Rogers, 1980, p. 160).

Trust is immutably related to genuine and real helping relationships. When we truly care for others, we trust them to maintain their independence, which includes the risk of allowing people to make mistakes. Doing for others what they are capable of doing for themselves or nurturing people to the degree that we satisfy our own insidious desires has the potential to create unhealthy, dependent relationships. In contrast, trusting relationships encourage people to develop fully while providing appropriate safeguards to ensure successful outcomes.

The genuineness and realness we convey in our helping relationships are to some degree related to the humility we have. When we behave in honest and genuine ways

Reflection

A graduate student in seminar once asked, "Can you care too much?" My first thought in responding was "Probably not." On further reflection, however, we both wondered, "If caring too much means overprotecting our clients and patients, then we might be doing them a disservice." What signals will you look for as a helping professional to avoid crossing the line of "caring too much?"

toward others and ourselves, we have no reason to pretend we are something other than what we are. Professional helpers understand this as acceptable ethical practice—to present themselves, their background, and their competencies to clients in an accurate manner. Volunteers and other helpers demonstrate similar ethics and humility by being genuine and accepting appropriate recognition for the work they perform and the contribution they make to the community. Most important, helpers maintain a balance between the accolades they receive that strengthen their self-worth and their understanding of the significant role other people play in their achievements and accomplishments. In this way, our humility is measured to the degree that we appreciate the contributions others make toward our success as helpers.

One characteristic of humility that we find among truly caring helpers is their ability to listen. In a previous work, I referred to this trait as the way people "listen with their eyes" (Schmidt, 1994). When we listen carefully to others, the message we send with our eyes says, "What you are saying is important to me," and as we continue in this mode of listening, we convey our level of understanding about their feelings. In a sense, we subjugate our own views and feelings to care deeply about the views and feelings of those to whom we are listening. Such modesty is a hallmark of a caring person.

Sometimes when we are busy in our professional role or become overwhelmed with the work at hand, we might be distracted by the situation or circumstances of the moment. When this happens, our ability to concentrate and listen fully to our clients could be diminished. Consequently, we might appear to behave in ways that indicate our work is more important than the people we are attempting to help. By placing our tasks above the welfare of our clients, we jeopardize the humility that we believe is an important ingredient in caring relationships.

A final aspect of humility is our understanding of the role our clients have in the success of any helping relationship. Although we bring specific knowledge and skill to the relationship, in the final analysis, it is the client who succeeds. Even in the most critical situation, where highly technical assistance, such as medical intervention, is paramount to a successful outcome, the client's willingness to respond and appropriately participate in the recovery process cannot be discounted. More accurately, the client's involvement must be considered essential to the success of any helping relationship.

Mayeroff (1971) offered two additional ingredients of caring—hope and courage—that together engender an optimistic posture in all helping relationships. In Chapter 4, we will consider the quality of optimism as an essential condition of the encouraging stance, an important intention of successful helpers. For now, we can define *hope* as the belief that beneficial outcomes in all our helping relationships will be realized both by us and by the people for whom we care. Such hope is not unrestrained optimism in which "anything is possible if only we believe." Rather, it is an unwavering confidence in the potential of the human spirit. It is also a genuine appreciation of the effect that hope has on strengthening people's willpower and determination to overcome what might seem like insurmountable challenges. At the same time, courage complements our hopefulness when caring for others because it sometimes takes a certain degree of nerve, heart, and fortitude to persevere with clients who struggle with difficult situations. As we encourage our clients to be brave and persevere, we are careful to protect them from unnecessary and unwise risk. In this sense, our caring is exemplified by being wisely courageous, meaning that we seek knowledge to ensure a safe course of action in all helping relationships.

ATTAINING SELF-KNOWLEDGE

All the ingredients of caring enumerated by Milton Mayeroff can be applied to relationships established by professional helpers. Each contributes in a significant way to the success of every relationship, and combined they define a truly caring relationship. To acquire these characteristics and apply them consistently and dependably in our helping relationships, we must first achieve a high level of knowledge about ourselves as helpers and about our particular field of professional service.

The act of caring, in a professional sense, assumes that the caregiver has a certain level of knowledge and expertise. At the same time, appropriate care can only be given if we, as helpers, have a healthy outlook, are self-confident, and have an accurate understanding of ourselves. These qualities enable us to establish healthy relationships with others, and they complement the expert knowledge required in all our helping. The most skilled technician, surgeon, behavioral counselor, or other helper who is void of the caring traits and qualities espoused here could be as much

Reflection

A mental health worker once reported how disappointed she was that most of her clients seemed to make so little progress; and when they did show some improvement, relapse seemed inevitable. We know that professional helpers are frequently challenged by the difficult situations their clients face. What has been your experience as a helper, and how would you respond to this colleague's disappointment?

a threat and hindrance to the well-being of clients and patients as he or she is a benefit to their development and healthfulness.

Helpers often work with clients to influence change in their lives. To attempt to influence change in other people without having the courage to examine and learn about ourselves seems misguided. If caring is an essential ingredient in our helping relationships, then learning about how and why we care seems to be an important step in becoming a successful caregiver.

Self-knowledge is a lifelong quest for all of us. As caring helpers, we learn about ourselves, our beliefs, and our values as well as how all these characteristics influence our caring behaviors. Understanding the importance of this self-knowledge is the first step to acquiring it. Once this appreciation is realized, the next step is to establish and maintain a process for self-reflection, self-monitoring, and self-development. An initial phase of the process is to reflect on our own development and assess how we have come to this point in our lives. For some of us, this may mean simply talking with family members about our childhood, reflecting on the values and beliefs we have retained from these early experiences, and examining those that might inhibit our performance as caring helpers.

For others of us, this assessment might require a formal helping relationship. This could include counseling or therapy to explore experiences and events that have helped carve a belief system that might not be as healthy as we would like. By seeking assistance for ourselves and exploring our own development, we illustrate our belief in the helping process and demonstrate the same courage we expect of those who someday might seek our assistance. Learning about our prejudices and confronting these biases, for example, show a willingness to rethink fundamental beliefs that are part of our being. Such action is courageous because for most of us it is scary to change our core beliefs and become someone different. Giving up long-held values means reshaping our self-concept and world view. It means letting go of fears, convictions, and opinions that have defined who we are. This is risky business because we are unsure how the emotions and beliefs that replace these perceptions will redefine us.

If counseling or therapy is not the process we choose for this self-examination, then two alternative avenues could help. The first is deep self-reflection to examine and change parts of our belief system that we find problematic. In a sense, the process involves peering through the looking glass, and it takes a high level of self-understanding and firm resolve to achieve these goals by ourselves. More likely, we will be assisted by incorporating a second process: asking close friends, family, and colleagues to react to our self-assessment and support our initiative to make changes in attitudes, behaviors, or other traits that we want to alter.

Self-examination and subsequent decisions to alter views and behaviors that are problematic in our effort to become more caring human beings is a sign of emotional health and well-being. Professional helpers and volunteers who take steps to improve their own lives are better equipped to care about others. Part of this process is to recognize the important role that encouragement from others plays in our own

Reflection

Have you ever had an experience that significantly altered beliefs you had held all your life? If so, reflect on this conversion and ask yourself whether you have some beliefs that restrict your ability to help people. How can you address these beliefs in ways that will remove them as obstacles to helping?

psychological and emotional health, especially encouragement from people we respect. For example, healthy professionals seek support beyond their day-to-day work environments to include a circle of friends or family members with whom they can confide and relate to on a personal level. Friendships can provide a valuable reflection of our beliefs and behaviors. When we are functioning in healthy ways, our friendships often mirror this beneficial posture. In contrast, when we are not performing in the most healthful ways, our closest friends will often gently confront us about our behavior and guide us to a healthier lifestyle.

Emotional well-being is connected to physical health. Successful helpers who want to care consistently about the welfare of their clients understand the impact that physical health has on their performance. Professional helpers are challenged by stressful situations; and if they are not in good physical condition, they may not always be able to provide the most caring service to those in need. By taking care of our physical selves, we are in better shape to cope with the stresses of being a professional or lay helper. We care about our diet, avoid overindulgence, exercise, watch our alcohol intake, quit smoking, and monitor our mental attitude to keep us in peak performance. All of these actions also contribute to an increased self-knowledge and understanding of who we are, which further strengthens our ability to care about others. In Chapter 5, we will explore this area of caring for ourselves in greater detail.

Helpers also enhance their self-knowledge by staying informed about their field of service. They attend workshops, read professional literature, create study groups, take classes, and join associations to improve knowledge and skill in their respective specialty. As an example, a school counselor who assists an adolescent with a parental divorce might want to examine recent counseling literature about how to help students who are struggling with a family breakup. By improving our knowledge and skill we build self-confidence, which is requisite for being a capable and caring helper.

UNDERSTANDING AND ACCEPTING OTHERS

When we have achieved a higher level of self-understanding and appreciation, we are in a stronger position to understand and accept others. This is the next area of demonstrating our care for others—attempting to understand fully and accept unconditionally the persons we try to help.

Previously, we explored the quality of empathy in caring relationships. Essential to our expression of empathy in all helping relationships is an understanding of the students, clients, or patients for whom we care. In addition, other aspects of caring, which we also examined, allow us to get closer to people so that we can become more accepting of who they are. Such acceptance is conveyed without judgment or evaluation; it is given unconditionally.

In this section, we will explore more fully what we mean by understanding and accepting the people we intend to help. The words *understanding* and *accepting* seem simple enough, and most people probably believe they comprehend their meaning. Yet in helping relationships, particularly those in which we want to express a deeper level of caring for other people, the notion of understanding and the act of accepting take on special significance.

Understanding can assume various forms and exist at different levels depending on the helping relationship being formed. In critical situations with little time for full explanation and discussion, our level of understanding about a client or patient might be minimal. For example, a clinical social worker confronted by a suicidal client might not have time to explore feelings at great depth or examine past experiences as contributing factors leading to the client's depression. Such a level of understanding may come later, but the social worker's immediate concern is to ensure the physical safety of the client and recognize the need for action.

Under less critical circumstances, we want to take time to understand fully the feelings and perceptions of the people we help. In these situations, it is important and appropriate to listen completely and make every effort to learn all about clients' concerns so that we fully appreciate their point of view. Describing this process in behavioral terms is difficult. To comprehend the idea of understanding our clients, we might examine what *not* to do rather than what we should do. For example, counselors cannot fully listen and understand their clients when they are distracted by phone calls and paperwork in front of them. By the same token, physicians cannot understand their patients' pain when they simply tell them what the symptoms mean in medical terminology. Likewise, a minister cannot fully understand a parishioner's dilemma if his or her response is to quote biblical passages or recite church doctrine. In sum, we will not reach full understanding with our clients and patients unless we devote full attention to them, listen without giving premature expert advice or information, and explore their feelings about the situation more deeply.

The understanding that is necessary in caring relationships is a form of sensitivity, which Combs and Gonzalez (1994) have noted "is essential for effective use of the helper's self" (p. 168). Therefore, to be successful as caring helpers, we must be sensitive to what clients bring us, how they view their individual situations, and, at the same time, resist the temptation to interject our perceptions and values into the helping relationship. The degree to which we interject our views, the level at which we self-disclose, and the frequency with which we provide expertise to our clients are all measures of our sensitivity or lack thereof. As such, they are also indicators of how effectively we control our *self* in the context of caring about others.

Accepting behaviors complement our understanding and sensitivity. They, too, are essential in establishing truly caring relationships. Acceptance is one of the core conditions that Carl Rogers put forth in his person-centered approach to therapy. He linked acceptance to unconditional positive regard, an attitude of creating a climate for change by first understanding the client's best intentions, respecting the client as he or she is, and empathizing with the problems and difficulties the client faces. For example, the therapist who is working with an alcoholic begins with the belief that the client wants to overcome this struggle with addiction and become a healthier, better-functioning person.

Most of us think of ourselves as accepting of others; but closer examination may discover that prejudices, biases, and fears prevent us from accepting all people as they are, without condition. This is a key factor in accepting others: we do it without setting conditions on the relationship.

When we think about them, we can see that most of our relationships in life are conditional. Friendships, colleagueships, love relationships, and countless other unions are often based on mutual benefit, even if they are not purely a quid pro quo understanding. Many of these conditional relationships are understandable because we each try to create safe havens for ourselves. Consequently, we search for associations in which we feel protected and have faith that people will treat us in the same manner as we treat them. In addition, most of us look for relationships that are familiar and comfortable. We associate with friends who have similar interests, initiate collegial relationships to achieve common goals, and establish loving relationships to satisfy the human need of personally being with others in deeply meaningful ways.

All these relationships can have aspects of caring even though we might retain some of the self-centered conditions that established them initially. Perhaps, as Rogers (1980), Mayeroff (1971), and others have suggested, these lifelong associations and unions might be stronger and healthier if we could sacrifice the conditions we set on them from the beginning. For example, if we could pursue all our friendships solely on the premise that we have much to contribute to the well-being of other people, we might find a larger, more fulfilling circle of friends. Such a stance takes courage and risk on our part because we must have faith in everyone with whom we establish close relationships.

Reflection

Remember a time in your life when you were not accepted by someone or by some group. As you recall this incident, think about the factors you might have controlled that could have altered the situation. Also think about factors that were out of your control. If you wanted to belong to this group or be accepted by this person today, what would you do?

Our professional and volunteer helping relationships are different from everyday friendships, marriages, partnerships, and other associations because of the lack of conditions we set on the acceptance of those people we aim to help. As noted, to be successful in these relationships, we accept students, clients, and patients unconditionally. This means we value them because they have worth in their own right, regardless of their life struggles or their apparently inappropriate behavior. This notion sounds simple and easy enough, but in practice we know how challenging it can be to put aside our own preferences and truly accept another human being. Yet without this high level of caring, we might not be able to establish consistently helpful relationships. To attain this level of acceptance, we examine the prejudices and fears that interfere with our performance. At the same time, we stay keenly aware of how our knowledge and skill, particularly our helping behaviors, are used in every relationship.

Professional helpers behave at high levels of caring and acceptance when they are aware of their verbal and nonverbal behaviors. This level of awareness relates to helper intentionality, a concept we will explore more completely in Chapter 2. For now, suffice it to say that helper intentionality is an inner guidance system that relates to a level of awareness regarding all our behaviors—what we intend to do and what we actually do in attempting to help others.

When we function at a high level of caring, we consistently choose behaviors that demonstrate our acceptance of others, regardless of who they are, where they come from, or how they behave. As such, we may not always agree with their ideas, the choices they want to make, or the behaviors they use to achieve their goals; but we care enough to listen, understand their point of view, and let them know we are willing to help in any way possible. Simultaneously, we use our knowledge and skill to encourage them to make responsible decisions about important life issues without imposing our values and beliefs on them. The ability to maintain this high level of acceptance while continuing to encourage clients and patients to make responsible choices is the sign of a truly artful helper—one who incorporates both the science and skill of helping with the art and grace of compassion and understanding.

At times, our students, clients, and patients appear to give up on themselves. For example, patients fighting difficult illnesses sometimes tire of the struggle and wonder if it is worth the pain and effort. Caring physicians, nurses, and other helpers encourage and challenge them to continue fighting. To behave in any other fashion, without challenging and confronting the patient, would be a sign of resignation and abandonment. Caring helpers do not avoid discord or difficult situations in search of more comfortable relationships. Instead, they use challenge and confrontation in a respectful manner to work toward positive outcomes in all relationships. We will explore the concepts of challenge and confrontation further in Chapter 2.

Caring helpers believe in their capabilities and have a high regard for the clients and patients they assist. As such, their own insecurities or biases do not govern them, nor are they directed by overly possessive and guileful wishes. Truly caring relationships are established on the firm belief that all people have intrinsic worth and that, given an understanding and accepting relationship, all people have the potential to develop as fully functioning and healthy human beings. This philosophy extends to all types of helping and across a realm of human interaction and caring.

REALMS OF CARING

Helping professionals and volunteers work in a variety of settings, and their acts of caring about and for clients can be categorized in a number of ways. Here, we consider three realms of caring: (1) as a professional function, (2) as an institutional responsibility, and (3) as a measure of personal and community commitment. Each realm has importance for professional and volunteer helpers. The first describes the inherent role that caring plays in helping relationships. The second presents the challenge of making sure that institutions, such as the schools, hospitals, and clinics where we serve our clients and patients, operate in the most caring and beneficial way possible. Lastly, caring is exemplified in the close, loving relationships we establish, in how we take care of our personal well-being, and in the community interest we maintain as helpers. As we proceed through this book, you might consider each realm and the role you could take as a professional or volunteer to ensure that intentional caring behaviors exist at optimal levels in all your relationships.

Caring As a Professional Function

Already in this chapter we have considered many aspects of caring that relate to how we function in our roles as helpers. Essential to being a caring professional are sound knowledge and adequate skill, but equally important are the attention and understanding we have for those who seek our assistance. Throughout this book, we will examine aspects of caring and their importance in every type of helping relationship. Your challenge is to determine how these aspects fit the unique professional arena in which you will serve clients and how to incorporate them into all your helping relationships. Meeting this challenge is fundamental to our ability to function in an intentional manner.

As noted, every helping relationship balances skill and knowledge applied by the helper with the ultimate care for the person being helped. If we use our skills and call on our expertise without careful regard for the patient's feelings and opinions, all our best intentions may lead to less than positive outcomes. By the same token, if we care deeply about our clients but fail to maintain a high level of skill and scientific practice, our irresponsibility may cause destruction rather than beneficial results. For example, a counselor might establish a comfortable, caring tone with a client who exhibits symptoms of depression; but if the counselor lacks skill and knowledge to prescribe proper treatment or initiate an appropriate referral, he or she might unwittingly precipitate a disastrous and possibly fatal outcome. Similarly, show us a loving, caring teacher who cannot individualize instruction or maintain classroom management, and we will find students who are not learning.

Intentional professionals and volunteers understand the important relationship and balance that exist between function and compassionate attachment in all their relationships. They strive to reach out, empathize, and care about their clients' welfare within the framework of skillful and knowledgeable practice.

Caring As an Institutional Responsibility

Helpers frequently work in organizations or institutions that offer a wide range of instructional, therapeutic, medical, and other services. With their employment or volunteer status comes the obligation to ensure that institutional policies and procedures are not developed and enacted at the expense of the clients who are being served. Sometimes schools, hospitals, and other agencies establish polices that are not in the best interest of their customers. For example, an elementary school that enforces a "no talking" policy during lunchtime does little to help children learn about proper etiquette or how to socialize appropriately during mealtimes. Instead of using the time for a positive learning experience, the policy places an extreme burden on teachers and assistants, who are charged with enforcing an unreasonable and impossible rule.

In an earlier work, William Purkey and I presented an assessment paradigm for counselors and other helpers to use when examining five factors that affect human interactions (Purkey & Schmidt, 1996). These factors are called the *Five P's:* people, places, policies, programs, and processes. In brief, these factors urge helpers to assess how their institutions treat the people they serve. We will return to these five factors later in this book to learn how to use them in an assessment process. By using the Five P's as an assessment model, institutions and organizations show they care about the people who depend on their services. In addition, helpers are better able to create places that are environmentally sound and aesthetically pleasing. They establish policies and design processes that put the customer first and implement programs that include all clients and patrons.

In a way, we can view institutions and organizations as living organisms. As such, they deserve the same caring attention that personal relationships deserve. When we tend to specific components of our schools, clinics, and other organizations—the people, places, policies, programs, and processes—we demonstrate a greater level of care for the people who receive our instruction, medical treatment, counseling, or other services. By keeping buildings clean, cultivating gardens to beautify grounds, maintaining facilities so they work properly, establishing nondiscriminating policies, and creating programs to monitor the health of the institution as a whole, we show a high level of regard for all involved. We will examine our role in helping institutions and agencies to become more responsive to clients and patients in the Chapter 6.

Caring As a Measure of Personal and Community Commitment

Our ability to create caring relationships with the clients and patients we serve is proportionate to the extent that we personally care for ourselves and those closest to us. In later chapters, we will explore in detail the connection between our own health and the ability we have to demonstrate caring for others. In addition, we will consider the importance of caring beyond professional functioning and examine the commitment we have to others and the community. Noted psychotherapist Alfred Adler called this aspect *Gemeinshaftsgefuhl*, or social interest (Sweeney, 1998). He posited that our emotional health is in large part related to the degree with which we express social interest, a willingness to belong, and a deep concern for community.

In this chapter, we have examined the quality of caring as an essential ingredient in all helping relationships. Caring is a multifaceted characteristic that involves understanding and acceptance of those whom we attempt to help. It is also predicated on the level of self-knowledge that we attain to ensure that our care for others is given responsibly and honorably. All these factors are interrelated and influenced by the purpose and direction we bring to every helping relationship. Understanding this purpose and direction is key to providing appropriate care. Purpose and direction, in turn, are guided by our *intentionality*—a construct that is fundamental to caring. If caring is the heart of helping, then intentionality is the mind and soul of how we behave in our helping relationships. In Chapter 2, we will examine the construct called intentionality and its relationship to effective helping and caring.

2

Intentionality and Caring

The possibilities emerge from the helper's assessment of the whole situation, using information about the person's cultural background . . . knowing the full range of methods appropriate to the goals of helping, and then selecting a response with confidence.

Lawrence M. Brammer
*The Helping Relationship:
Process and Skills,* 1993, p. 44

Helping relationships generate seemingly limitless choices for counselors, nurses, social workers, and other practitioners. Helping clients to make personal decisions, responding to a patient's allergic reaction to medication, and finding financial assistance for a family in crisis are among the countless relationships that professional helpers establish. In its own unique way, each presents an array of choices. Sometimes the choices appear clear and definite, while at other times we are less certain of what to do or which way to go with students, clients, or patients. This variance notwithstanding, effective helpers know that all the choices they make, from least to most important, invariably play a role in the overall success of every helping relationship.

Successful counseling, nursing practice, and other helping relationships are seldom achieved by accident or coincidence. More likely, a successful helping relationship is the product of preparation and action intertwined with caring and essential knowledge. An important ingredient of these relationships is the helper's purposeful effort, which is put forth in all interactions. This willing effort is orchestrated with the intention of helping clients and others make decisions, live healthfully, and become successful at handling life's challenges. Successful helpers assess situations, identify treatment goals, develop appropriate interventions, and incorporate into these processes a level of caring appropriate for each relationship. The combined process of assessing situations, setting goals, and choosing interventions with utmost care relies on the helper's intentions. These intentions—thoughts, desires, beliefs,

21

and behaviors—form the *intentionality* of the helper, a construct inextricably linked with the process of caring.

In this chapter, we will explore helper intentionality and its connection with all our caring relationships. We will see how it guides empathy, functioning as an inner structure that enables us to give direction and purpose to our professional relationships. As such, our intentionality guides the overall way in which we manifest our caring and understanding in all helping relationships.

INTENTIONALITY

Since the beginning of civilization, philosophers and theologians have studied human intentionality. In the past few decades, this construct has gained the attention of helping professionals. Existential therapist Rollo May (1969) viewed intentionality as a critical element related to successful therapy. He maintained that people's perceptions are always influenced by their intentions; and since intentionality is the basis for these purposes, it provides the framework by which people organize and interpret what they see happening around them.

May (1969) credited the philosopher Aristotle with saying, "What is given to the eyes is the intention of the soul." One paraphrase of Aristotle's observation is "People see what they have a mind to see." By extending this translation, we can define *intentionality* as the control people have of their purpose and direction in life. This control is strongly influenced by the way in which people see themselves and by their perceptions of the world around them. In a helping relationship, the phenomenon is true for both the helper and the client. Therefore, counselors, nurses, and other practitioners are influenced by their experiences and subsequent perceptions in every helping relationship they enter. Their view of the client's physical, psychological, and social persona as well as their own perception of the presenting problem or situation are related to their own intentionality. This interaction between the intentionality of the helper and the intentionality of the client allows the relationship to become a dynamic process.

According to May (1969), intentionality is "the structure which gives meaning to experience" (p. 223). He traced its philosophical and epistemological roots from the writings of several philosophers, including St. Thomas Aquinas, Immanuel Kant, and Franz Bretano, and to the later works of Edmund Husserl and Martin Heidegger. May

Reflection

Sometimes the purpose of the helper appears to be in conflict with the purpose of the client. Resolving this conflict is paramount to successful helping. In your field of professional helping, what ethical guidelines apply when you find yourself involved in such conflicts?

believed that the word derives from the Latin *intendere* and *tensum*, thus illustrating the "stretching toward," "taking care of," and "purposeful" meanings the construct conveys. He viewed intentionality as the ability of people to link their inner consciousness and perceptions with their mindful intentions and overt behaviors. By this definition, he posited that intentionality "is not to be identified with intentions, but it is the dimension which underlies them; it is man's capacity to have intentions" (1969, p. 224). As such, the intentionality of counselors, therapists, nurses, and other helping professionals is a foundation for caring. It is our capacity to reach out, take care of, and tend to others in purposeful ways.

Intentionality, as defined here, has implications for the characteristics of caring and empathy as well as for the qualities of direction and purpose. Our intentionality allows us to form intentions based on our perceptions of helping and enables us to use these intentions to move our helping relationships through various phases toward successful conclusions.

Intentionality has also been viewed as a preconscious process that leads to human interaction (Bugental, 1980). When we think about our wishes and desires and move toward action to realize these goals, we illustrate how intentionality is an unconscious foundation (what May refers to as "inner consciousness") for human interaction. According to Bugental (1980), as people move through this process successfully, they achieve a sense of worth and "the power of *being*, reaching forward to *becoming*" (p. 56). Applying this understanding to helping relationships, we can suppose that everything we, as helpers, choose to say or do is guided by our intentionality, which enables us to control what happens in our effort to assist others.

Searle (1983) explained that intentions are part of the broader notion of intentionality and differentiated the concept from human consciousness. He noted that intentions, such as a counselor's behaviors in therapy, belong to a larger construct that offers direction and meaning to the helping relationship. Analogous to Bugental's view, Searle also asserted that a person's conscious awareness of internal intentions (e.g., thoughts and feelings) does not necessarily signify a high degree of intentionality. Thus, a helper might be fully aware of his or her feelings and still behave in unintentional ways toward certain clients. For example, a psychiatric nurse might be aware that his long hours on the ward have brought on fatigue, yet that awareness does not enable him to control an abrupt and uncaring response to a patient's request for assistance.

Although there is general agreement about the concept of intentionality and its relationship to internal mental states, philosophers, psychologists, and other scholars

Reflection

Sometimes even our awkward attempts at helping are successful in large part because our clients are accurate in reading the genuineness of our intentions. What do you think about people's ability to read the intentions of others?

do not always agree on some of its basic components. According to Noel (1993), these differences cover a full spectrum of views that are familiar to counselors, therapists, and other professional helpers. At one end lies the perspective that people have thoughts, beliefs, feelings, and other internal states that influence how they behave. At the other end is the strict behavioral view that declines to accept inner states on the premise that such constructs cannot be observed or measured and therefore have no meaning.

In this book, we take the position that an understanding of caring and its important role in helping relationships embraces the first perspective on the spectrum. This position is consistent with the philosophy put forth by early pioneers in the helping professions and more recently expressed in the counseling literature (e.g., Combs & Gonzalez, 1994; Ivey & Ivey, 1998; Purkey & Schmidt, 1996). Research findings have emphasized the importance of understanding our own inner beliefs and thoughts as helpers to better empathize with people. Combs and Gonzalez (1994) summarized those results:

> In the research, good helpers were characterized by continuous concern for the "people" question—immediate understandings about how things seem to the person involved. Poor helpers were preoccupied with "things" questions—external matters, pressures, power, possessions, and the historical details of how matters came to present state. (p. 22)

Studies generally demonstrate that successful helpers tend to exhibit positive perceptions of self and others, are personally motivated and fully functioning, show an accurate awareness of the world, and use this insight to facilitate beneficial helping relationships. Therefore, awareness and insight, combined with knowledge of the skills to apply in a particular helping relationship, are relevant to the helper's intentionality.

In recent years, intentionality has received increased attention as an essential variable for counselors and other helpers who function successfully (Hamer, 1995; Ivey & Ivey, 1998; Purkey & Schmidt, 1996). For example, Allen Ivey (Ivey & Ivey, 1998) sees intentionality as a broad construct underlying the goals of helping and explains how capable helpers are able to generate alternate behaviors, strategies, and interventions

Reflection

An important aspect of our development as helpers is the ability to assess our self-perceptions, awareness of the world around us, and personal insight. When tested against the views of family, friends, and colleagues we respect, this self-assessment places us in a strong position to apply our knowledge and skills in an intentionally helpful manner. Whom do you rely on to validate your views about professional helping?

to respond to clients' needs at various moments in the helping relationship. As noted, intentionality enables helpers to establish a consistent direction with a careful purpose and a dependable posture for assisting people who seek their help.

Ivey and Ivey (1998) have defined *intentionality* as "acting with a sense of capability and deciding from a range of alternative actions. The intentional individual has more than one action, thought, or behavior to choose from in responding to changing life situations" (p. 14). Therefore, helpers who behave with a high degree of intentionality respond to different challenges and unpredictable situations without becoming trapped in a single response mode. They avoid using one skill, a single definition of the problem, and one approach to interviewing. To be a successful professional helper means evaluating situations thoroughly, choosing from several options, offering clients reasonable alternatives, and interviewing in an appropriate manner to fit the given relationship.

In his self-concept approach to understanding human relationships, William Purkey described intentionality as a bipolar concept (Purkey & Novak, 1996). According to this view, human intentionality consists of two poles: one of helpful behaviors, a second of harmful behaviors. Between these two poles lies *unintentionality*, an unclear and uncertain area that contributes either to inconsistent, thoughtless, and careless behaviors or to serendipitously fortuitous outcomes. Accordingly, everyone functions at some point on the continuum of intentionality. People behave in intentionally harmful or helpful ways and in unintentional ways, depending on their perceptions of particular situations and the responses they choose in each circumstance.

The analogy of stretching a rubber band might help us to understand this bipolar view of intentionality, particularly the notion of unintentionality. When stretched, the rubber band represents the full continuum of intentionality. The two ends that we hold represent the strongest and most intentional of our behaviors. The weakest point is the center of the rubber band, which stretches and tears as it is pulled in opposite directions. The center of the band has no direction of its own. Consequently, according to this analogy, the middle of the rubber band is unintentional in its direction and purpose.

Figure 2.1 illustrates the bipolar aspect of intentionality. It illustrates the positive and negative dimensions of intentionality as well as its uncertain dimension—*unintentionality*. Furthermore, the diagram can be used to show the perceptions, experiences, and beliefs that influence a person's intentionality at both ends of the continuum. It is these components that guide our purpose in every helping relationship.

Figure 2.1 shows human behavior moving in one of two directions away from unintentionality. On the helpful side, the diagram depicts caring, giving, and assisting as three examples of positive directions. At times, the arrow indicates a return toward unintentionality, thus illustrating the human condition of imperfection. It is natural for people to behave unintentionally at times, even when they do so in a helpful manner.

On the opposite side of unintentionality, the figure shows punishing, hurting, and taking as three harmful directions. At the same time, the arrow again tries to return to an unintentional purpose. Even the most destructive personality can behave in helpful ways, although it may not intend to do so.

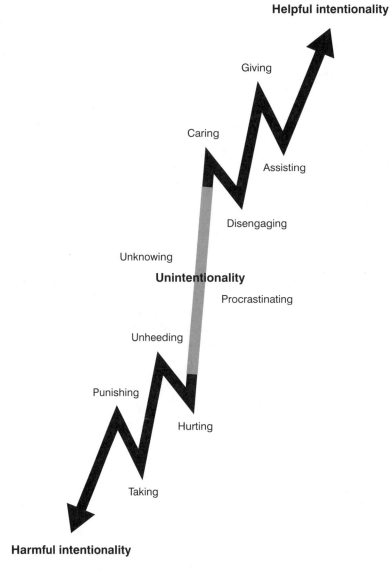

Helpful intentionality

Giving

Caring

Assisting

Disengaging

Unknowing

Unintentionality

Procrastinating

Unheeding

Punishing

Hurting

Taking

Harmful intentionality

FIGURE 2.1 *Bipolarity of intentionality*

It is rare to find helpers who are so fraudulent that they consistently intend to do harm. More often, we discover helpers who behave in unintentional ways. The figure illustrates these types of behaviors as unknowing, disengaging, procrastinating, and unheeding. Helpers who function primarily in an unintentional manner might sometimes be successful with clients and patients. However, it is dangerous to behave this way most of the time because helpers are unlikely to repeat successful relationships if they do not know what worked.

A more serious risk in being unintentional is the potential for harm. Even if they are well intended, inaccurate diagnoses, invalid assessments, and untested interventions might do irreparable damage to students, clients, or patients.

Intentionality is an internal power that allows us to give direction and meaning to our behaviors. As helpers, then, we give clear direction and purpose to relationships to the degree that we are aware and in control of our intentions. When we function with a high degree of intentionality while demonstrating true caring and genuine empathy toward those who seek our assistance, we are able to control our behaviors and, to a large extent, the consequences of our actions. Without such awareness and command of our helping behaviors, we risk being unintentional, which, as noted, does not gives us clear direction or dependability with our clients.

Counselors, social workers, and other professional helpers who falter with their dependability might not achieve a level of confidence and credibility with the people they attempt to help. Moreover, when confronted or threatened by others because of their unreliability, some professionals may resort to destructive and harmful behaviors as a means of defending their self-worth. For example, a mental health counselor who makes an inaccurate diagnosis and is confronted by the client's family members might resort to attacking their integrity and blaming them for the difficult situation. Such behavior, resulting from what was initially unintentional functioning, has now regressed to a level of unprofessional and perhaps unethical practice.

As mentioned, we rarely find professionals who work as helpers in the community yet use their positions for negative, destructive purposes. It is difficult to explain why people would assume such a dishonest role, but sadly it does happen. In these instances, we might conclude that the person is behaving in an intentionally harmful manner because some social dysfunction, hostility, ignorance, or pathology is interfering with healthy life goals. For example, when a therapist violates ethical standards and takes sexual advantage of a vulnerable client, he or she makes that decision with specific direction and purpose, neither of which is helpful to the client.

Because our intentionality influences the selection of positive and negative behaviors, it can be either a constructive or destructive force in the establishment of helping relationships. Counselors, psychologists, and other professionals who understand the power inherent in being a helper recognize that what they decide to

Reflection

Have you ever driven your car to work or school, parked, and then wonder how you got there? Sometimes our behaviors become so automatic, so unconscious, that we have no memory of doing them. What are the implications of such automation for helping?

do, or not to do, with their clients is either the catalyst for psychotherapy or the driving force for psychopathology. As Purkey and Schmidt (1996) commented, professional helpers "can be a beneficial presence, or a lethal one, in the lives of their clients" (p. 54). Again, we emphasize that for most professional helpers the common danger to our effectiveness is not so much the intent to be destructive as our *unintentions* in using the knowledge and skills we have learned. It is our inconsistency in being intentionally helpful. When we use our knowledge and skill in the most caring manner, we approach the highest level of intentional helping.

INTENTIONAL HELPING

Chapter 1 explained the meaning of caring and its importance in developing truly helpful relationships. The dimensions that define caring are influenced by our intentionality as helpers—the inner voice that guides our choices on behalf of, and in support of, people who seek our assistance. Indeed, these conditions are powerful factors in all helping relationships. Sidney Jourard (1964) noted that everyone's well-being is greatly affected by the degree to which each individual finds meaning, direction, and purpose in life. Similarly, a helper's intentions are a measure of successful relationships when genuine caring complements clear direction and purpose.

Successful professional helpers know that purpose and direction are insufficient qualities for beneficial relationships because, in and of themselves, these two ingredients do not require the essential core conditions of helping. Without an appropriate level of caring and sincere empathy, direction can lead to purposes that are not always in the best interest of clients. In the extreme, such purposes may serve the wishes and desires of a fraudulent clinician, an indifferent institution, or a malicious benefactor. These kinds of relationships might result in destructive or even lethal consequences.

At the same time, the destruction left in the wake of unintentional counselors, teachers, medical professionals, and others shows that a lack of direction and purpose, especially when caring qualities are also absent, will not result in beneficial relationships. For example, a former graduate student once told me that a high school counselor laughed openly at the student's wish to attend college. Even though the counselor responded thoughtlessly and therefore unintentionally, this careless act delayed the student's entry to college because of the residual self-doubt it inflicted.

Although caring plays an essential role in helping, successful helpers must also maintain a consistent direction and purpose in their working relationships. In contrast, misdirected or undirected relationships are rarely, if ever, productive. Thus, direction and purpose, while not sufficient qualities, are nonetheless essential to establishing successful helping relationships. At this point, it is necessary to examine direction and purpose more closely.

Knowing What

Direction means knowing what to do in helping situations. Carl Rogers (1951) developed his client-centered approach (today called "person-centered") as a nondirective method of therapy, as opposed to approaches that seem helper-oriented and give direct instruction, guidance, and assistance. But is any helping process truly void of direction? Perhaps the descriptions *nondirective* and *directive* approaches are misnomers. Rogers was a renowned counselor whose research and theory has had immeasurable impact on the helping professions (Beutler, Machado, & Neufeldt, 1994). His work has not only been studied by every counselor and many other professional helpers, but videotapes of his helping skills have been viewed by nearly all students preparing to be counselors, psychotherapists, or psychologists. What one gleans from the study of Rogers's contribution is a not so much a lack of direction in the helping process but a direction that is chosen as much by the client as by the professional helper. So when a person-centered counselor listens and reflects what the client is saying, the responses are given with a high level of intentionality, encouraging the client to find a direction within the helping relationship.

According to Patterson and Hidore (1997), "one of the oldest misconceptions about client-centered or relationship therapy is that the therapist is a purely passive participant in the process. The use of the term *nondirective* with reference to the therapist may have encouraged this view" (pp. 169–170). They suggest that a better term might be *noncontrolling* because the intent is to focus on the client's responsibility for deciding the content and direction of the therapeutic process. "The therapist is far from being a passive participant. His or her responsibility is to actively create an environment that minimizes threat so that the client is free to work without the restrictions that occur under conditions of personal threat" (p. 170).

By definition, the progress we hope to see in any helping relationship gives direction to the process. Therefore, a relationship that wanders endlessly without moving in a positive and beneficial direction can hardly be called "helping." In truly helpful relationships, counselors, nurses, and other professionals give utmost care to ensure progress toward goals that their clients have identified. What each helper contributes to a successful relationship is his or her *knowledge* and *skill* used with genuine empathy. In other words, true caring insists on knowledgeable, skilled practices.

It makes sense that successful helpers know what to do when they establish helping relationships. They are in charge of their behaviors, are focused on specific goals, and take responsibility for their actions. At the same time, they have a knowledge base that enables them to facilitate relationships in which the people they are attempting to assist can also identify goals, explore barriers, choose behaviors to overcome obstacles, and assume responsibility for the outcome of their decisions.

Reflection

Sometimes helpers become frustrated because they "struggle to help their clients see the problem." Do you note a fundamental flaw in their approach that is contributing to their frustration?

Unfortunately, many people who seek the assistance of professional helpers exist in relationships that might be described as a stalemate with themselves. They do not know what to do or what they want in life. Professional helpers often listen to these common expressions from clients: "I don't know what I am going to do about my marriage." "What can I do to make my career more satisfying?" "My life is unfulfilled."

Intentional helpers recognize the importance of current knowledge in all their helping relationships. They also understand that this knowledge is multifaceted. It includes skills that enable them to move each relationship in a positive direction and incorporates an understanding of various approaches to helping and the research findings that provide the underpinning for these approaches. At the same time, this knowledge includes practical information specific to the problems or issues presented by their clients. This broad knowledge base distinguishes professionals from lay helpers who are successful in large part because of their natural inclination to reach out and care for others.

Natural inclinations to care for others are essential ingredients for both lay and professional helpers. As such, they are not to be taken for granted, nor should they be casually dismissed. What distinguishes natural-born helpers from professional helpers is not the degree of empathy and concern they have for other people but the level of knowledge and skill they bring to specific helping relationships. Knowing what to do in specific situations influences our overall intentionality and subsequent success as helpers. Although this assumption is speculative, research of helper effectiveness indicates that skillful use of approaches may be an important element to consider. For example, Sexton and Whiston (1991) reviewed several studies and found that, when measured from a client's perspective, the more a counselor conveys empathy, the more likely a positive outcome will be realized. At the same time, however, their analysis shows that the helping process is enhanced when counselors skillfully help clients focus on goals and explore pertinent issues and experiences. They surmised: "It is not the school of thought but the skillfulness of the counselor and a number of aspects of the counseling process . . . that may be most important in successful counseling" (p. 344). This conclusion supports the notion that caring and other essential conditions of helping relationships, when combined with the knowledge and skill of a trained professional, increase the likelihood of positive outcomes.

An emphasis on balancing caring behaviors with our knowledge and skill does not diminish Gilbert Wrenn's (1973) observation more than a quarter-century ago: "To me the most striking personal discovery of the past decade has been that people respond to my degree of caring more than to my degree of knowing" (p. 249). People do seem to respond more to our caring than they do to what we know. The research supports this observation in terms of clients' perceptions (Combs & Gonzalez, 1994). Nevertheless, in a professional sense helpers attend to additional research findings that indicate it is the combined influence of caring and other core conditions conveyed with skillful and knowledgeable practice that generate positive outcomes in helping relationships.

At this point, it may be helpful to examine areas of knowledge that we might apply to the concept of "knowing what." Helping professionals work with a wide range of clients in a variety of educational, medical, and clinical settings. As such, the areas of necessary knowledge are often extensive. It is impractical, however, to expect helpers to maintain a fluid command and understanding of all the knowledge necessary to help every client who seeks their assistance. For example, a clinical social worker whose main area of expertise is working with abusive families may not have expertise in attention deficit disorder (ADD), which affects some children. In such a situation, the social worker needs to recognize the limits of his or her competency, know where to find accurate information about ADD, and know where to refer the child and family for additional services when necessary.

In this example, we note three areas of knowledge that apply to all helping relationships. The first is knowledge of the basic skills and competencies needed in the helping process. These skills must also be related to knowledge of particular approaches to helping. A second area of knowledge is specific information and understanding of content that are relevant to particular helping relationships. As discussed, these content areas are numerous and in some cases extensive. For example, professional counselors may have expertise in childhood, adolescent, or adult development or may focus their practice on personal adjustment, educational, or career counseling.

A third knowledge base is an understanding of processes to use in locating information, particularly about a content area that may be beyond a helper's expertise. Where do therapists and other helpers look for information that may be beneficial to clients and their helping relationships? If such information is not readily available or if its acquisition is insufficient to enable the helper to assist a client, then knowledge of other avenues, such as a referral to another professional, is required.

Knowing Why

If understanding our clients' goals and knowing what to do in order to help clients reach their objectives enable us to maintain direction, then knowing why gives purpose to all our helping relationships. Taking command of this purpose and ensuring that every relationship maintains a positive direction are pivotal aspects of helper intentionality and ones that encompass a caring quality.

Counselors, social workers, and other helpers demonstrate high intentionality and ultimate caring when the knowledge they apply and the purpose of their intentions are used primarily for the benefit and welfare of their clients and the common good of society. While this statement may sound utopian, professional helpers and volunteers always work within the context of an institution—for example, in a school

Reflection

> Assess your knowledge of the particular professional arena in which you plan to practice. What do you know and what do you still need to learn?

Reflection

Why do you want to help others? How aware are you of the overall purpose that underpins your desire to help?

or a larger organization, such as a mental health system. As discussed, these institutions and systemic organizations sometimes put in place programs and policies that hinder the establishment of helping relationships that are in the best interest of particular clients (Purkey & Schmidt, 1996). For example, a school policy that forbids students to receive counseling services during instructional periods might cause counselors to schedule sessions when students are less likely to take advantage of this assistance. The intentional counselor who truly cares about student welfare could first intervene by working to change the school's policy. Instructional time is important; but if particular students are not learning because of personal, social, and other difficulties that could be addressed through counseling, then the counselor might advocate for a change in policy that allows some flexibility in students' schedules.

Other times, personal needs and professional preferences of the helper may supercede the best interests of a student, client, or patient. For instance, a therapist who hastily determines that behavior modification techniques will be useful because they are easy for the client to learn and will expedite the sessions might apply the strategy without clear consent and understanding. What began as a helping relationship may soon appear to be manipulation or, worse, coercion. Although the therapist knows what to do in terms of the skill needed for the behavioral strategy, the *purpose* of the relationship may have moved from a positive direction to one of convenience and expediency. When helpers use strategies and choose their behaviors simply to satisfy organizational policy or adhere to a particular approach without full consideration and care for the people they are attempting to help, the purpose of these relationships is suspect at best. Purkey and Schmidt (1996) referred to this dichotomy of purpose as the difference between "doing to" and "doing with" in counseling and other helping relationships.

In "doing to" relationships, the helper sculpts, molds, and otherwise manipulates the environment so that the client can be expected to respond in a certain way. The hope of such machination—and, on occasion, deception—is to change the client's behavior and is done without due consideration of and collaboration with the client. Studies of social exchange theory (Molm, 1997) find that the use of coercion is difficult. Control of consistency and contingencies is rare, so "consequently, we should expect greater variability in the effectiveness of coercion and more ineffective use of coercion in general" (p. 268).

In the example just given, we might conclude that such a "doing to" posture moves beyond the application of accepted behavioral approaches, which when used in a caring manner include informed consent, understanding, voluntary participation, and full involvement of the client. An example of an acceptable behavioral approach that diminishes the "doing to" philosophy might be teaching relaxation techniques to help a client cope with anticipated anxiety involving work-related stress. In such a relationship, the therapist would seek the client's consent, explain the rationale for the strategy, teach the essential techniques, and practice the intervention with the client.

Helpers who embrace a "doing with" relationship view their clients as equal partners. They seek agreement and commitment for every strategy and intervention selected and value true collaboration with each client. Most important, helpers who adopt a "doing with" approach are in a stronger position to appreciate the full impact of intentionality on the helping relationship. They understand that intentions can embody a full range of human behaviors, from the cruelest and most destructive to the most kindhearted and caring. As we have discussed, this is a bipolar perspective of human intentionality (Purkey & Schmidt, 1996)—a perspective that cautions us, as helpers, about the power we possess to help or harm the people who seek our assistance. In Chapter 6 we will revisit this concept of "doing with" when we explore loving relationships.

The positive and negative potential of helping relationships might be a frightening concept for novices or students who are being prepared as professional helpers. Counselors, nurses, social workers, and other professionals have knowledge and skill to be a valuable influence in the lives of other people. When such knowledge and skill are misused, the outcome can have a profound and devastating effect. Or, as noted, when command of knowledge and skills is uncertain or unclear, the unintentional results lead to ineffective relationships. Therefore, for the novice helper as well as the veteran, the key is to stay focused on the *what* and the *why* of their relationships. Effective helping involves more than having a good heart or well-meaning intentions; those qualities must be applied knowledgeably, skillfully, and consistently. Truly caring professionals use their knowledge and training to keep the best interest of their clients in mind while working to better serve the entire community. They understand that, to be an effective helper, they must balance their care with themselves, their clients, and the larger society.

BALANCING CARE

Balance is important in all aspects of our lives, so it makes sense that successful helpers are aware of its significance in their helping relationships. Helpers who focus all their energy on caring for others without regard for their own health and welfare may not have the energy or capacity to provide quality services. At the same time, helpers who neglect or ignore how their actions make a difference or detract from the greater good of society might have too narrow a focus to be truly beneficial to their clients. In contrast, intentional helpers realize that their success with one client multiplies when that client reaches out and helps another person in need.

If intentionality is a key ingredient for successful helping and genuine caring, it follows that intentional helpers try to find balance in their personal and professional lives. The hypothesis is that we are most effective as caregivers when we balance our

Reflection

In helping relationships, clients draw conclusions about their helper's intentions. These conclusions may or may not be accurate, but the client thinks they are true. Who knows the true intentions of the helper?

attention and efforts in ways that take care of ourselves so we can better serve our clients and the community at large. A contrasting assumption is that, without adequate balance in the care we give to others, society, and ourselves, the help we offer will have neither a consistently clear direction nor a dependably beneficial purpose. For example, when professionals and volunteers focus so much energy and time on helping clients and people in need, they might neglect their responsibilities at home. Consequently, the resulting family stressors might diminish the likelihood of being successful in either venue. A volunteer emergency squad member who spends all her time answering calls, maintaining equipment, and attending school to update skills to the point where her family responsibilities suffer puts her children and marriage at risk. In time, the added stress could detract from the successful volunteer work she performs for the community.

The degree of intentionality we maintain contributes to our ability to have a realistic balance in the care we provide. The effort we devote to helping others influences the balance of energy we have left to offer family, colleagues, friends, and ourselves. For this reason, it is essential that we intentionally orchestrate direction, purpose, and balance in our personal and professional lives.

Helpers who maintain balance and create healthy lives for themselves behave in ways that benefit their mental, physical, and emotional health and thus are in much better form to help others. Healthy helpers recognize the importance of keeping fit so that the mind and body can cope with the challenges and stresses of caring for others. They are psychologically healthy people who understand the importance of physical fitness in forming effective helping relationships (Collingwood, 1976; Hinkle, 1988). Physical, mental, and emotional health, therefore, are examples of how helpers must focus on their own well-being to care adequately for others.

Finally, because professional helpers are often employed by organizations, agencies, and schools, we balance our loyalty and commitment to the institutions we rep-

Reflection

Assess your balance as a caring helper by measuring your (1) physical fitness, (2) emotional health, (3) social well-being, and (4) educational preparation. How well do you measure up to other helpers you know?

resent and the communities we serve. Institutions consist of mission statements, policies, regulations, and other aspects that might not always be in the best interest of individual clients. For example, a school system's testing program, implemented simply to demonstrate how different schools compare, might not consider the negative effects on individual students, teachers, and others involved. A counselor in the school might be challenged to provide appropriate services that help students deal with their individual feelings about testing performance and support teachers in trying to use test data to strengthen curriculum and instruction. At the same time, the counselor has a professional obligation to help the school system make sound choices in designing and implementing its testing program.

Likewise, communities often levy taxes, pass ordinances, or take other actions that, although intended to help all people, might have a negative impact on particular individuals or groups. A youth activist might become discouraged, for example, if the town council cuts its after-school and evening recreational programs for adolescents due to budget constraints. In this one decision, the council might undo years of work that has provided constructive activity to help young people learn social skills and keep them out of trouble.

The primary purpose of caregivers in all settings is to help individuals and groups learn, overcome obstacles, and succeed in a variety of ways. Such intentionality, however, is always influenced, positively or negatively, by social structures and the settings in which we practice. The choices we make to address these influences become part of our intentionality and consequently have an important role in how we balance our allegiance with the institutions and communities that employ us with the care we provide for others.

When we become unbalanced in our caring, we may operate at an extreme level of unintentionality. On such occasions, we might realize the predicament and ask ourselves, "What happened?" "What was I thinking?" Sometimes we might not take responsibility for this imbalance but blame others: "Why didn't you say something to me?" If people respond, "We tried to tell you, but you would not listen," we might argue, "Well, you didn't try hard enough!" Blaming others is another illustration of how our unintentionality can sometimes lead us toward harmful behaviors and relationships.

When we maintain a balance of intentional direction and purpose, we are better able to take caring relationships to greater heights. In such helping roles, we continually and consistently encourage others and ourselves to move in a positive direction. We seek conventional and unconventional methods of supporting others in the quest for self-actualization. As William Glasser (1965), a noted author and the founder of reality therapy, reminded us, we never give up.

ENCOURAGING, SUPPORTING, PERSEVERING

Intentional helpers use countless methods and strategies to encourage and support their clients and other people. Sometimes this support is given actively and overtly. Tutoring a student, attending a patient's musical performance, driving an injured person to the emergency room, or shopping for a sick friend are some examples. At other times, support and encouragement may be more subtle. For example, body language, facial expressions, and other signals can demonstrate support and encouragement. A friendly smile or a nod of agreement, for example, lets people see our support.

When we are aware of how our verbal and nonverbal behaviors support and encourage others, we function at a high level of intentionality. Consequently, we demonstrate a dependable level of caring toward all people with whom we have contact. Furthermore, we understand that to function at a high level of caring, we consistently choose behaviors that encourage and support others. Such encouragement and support might not always indicate agreement with the choices of our clients, patients, or students, but we understand that caring often requires us to risk letting people make their own decisions.

As we learned in Chapter 1, support and encouragement may take the form of challenge and confrontation. When people are faced with difficulty in their lives, they sometimes are tempted to give up the struggle. Intentional helpers demonstrate their true caring when they challenge and confront behaviors such as negative thinking and surrender. To allow clients and patients to give up without dispute is equivalent to resignation and abandonment. Clients who would rather give up might resist our efforts and resort to anger, threats, or other hostile behaviors. This is a time for persistence on our part even though it may be uncomfortable to everyone involved. As caring counselors and other practitioners, we do not avoid conflict simply because it is more comfortable to do so. We understand that by challenging and confronting certain clients, we demonstrate high regard and respect, which eventually lead to positive outcomes in helping relationships.

Sometimes helping relationships become stymied: clients make little progress toward their goals or, worse, regress to past problematic behavior. When this happens, our caring may take the form of challenge or confrontation, which is not to be interpreted as a lack of acceptance of our clients. Rather, when used with utmost care and respect for a client's unique perspective, challenge and confrontation can be clear signs of acceptance and understanding. "Challenge, confrontation, exhortation, and other actions that inspire, persuade, dare, and otherwise expect people to improve their lives are important invitations" (Schmidt, 1996, p. 36). To be truly helpful, however, we create and send such messages from a perspective of high regard, unconditional acceptance, and genuine concern for the client's welfare.

Patterson and Hidore (1997) affirmed this understanding of confrontation in a therapeutic relationship. They noted that the typical dictionary definition of *confrontation* includes the notion of hostility and conflict between two people. In helping relationships, however, confrontation is not about conflict between the client and helper but a way of pointing out discrepancies between what our clients say they want to see happen and the behaviors they choose that may inhibit them from reaching these goals. In helping relationships, therefore, confrontation is an attempt to help clients become more aware of the incongruity that exists among their feelings, attitudes, behaviors, and other factors surrounding their current situation.

One caveat about support is necessary. At times, what appears to be supportive behavior in helping relationships may result in undesirable outcomes. This may happen because we confuse support with overprotection. Subsequently, our clients become overly dependent on us as helpers. In these instances, the support is out of balance, and the helper is unintentionally taking responsibility for behaviors and decisions that belong to clients. Such actions may be intended as caring support, but in reality they deny clients the opportunity to develop and become responsible for their own welfare.

Lastly, intentional support and encouragement include the quality of perseverance. Successful helping relationships are often the result of our steadfast commitment to see clients reach their goals. Such persistence demonstrates resolve within the helping process and faith in a client's ability to succeed. It also seems to be a requisite to caring. People who refuse to give up in their attempts to help others, regardless of challenges and seemingly insurmountable odds, exhibit all the qualities of caring that we have considered thus far in this book. In addition, they most likely have an inner structure that enables them to be consistent with their caring relationships.

In this chapter we explored the construct of intentionality and learned how knowledge and skill interact with our ability to maintain direction and purpose in helping students, clients, and patients. We also learned that caring is an essential component for keeping our intentionality on a beneficial track. In Chapter 3, we will delve deeper into the structure and form of caring—the anatomy, if you will—and explore how our perceptions relate to our level of understanding and use of knowledge and helping skills.

$\mathcal{3}$

Anatomy of Intentional Caring

It is impossible to accurately sense the perceptual world
of another person unless you value that person and his
or her world—unless you, in some sense, care.

Carl Rogers
A Way of Being, 1980, p. 152

If caring consists of the various qualities examined in Chapter 1 and intentionality brings purpose and direction to our caring behaviors, it follows that we can design a structure to explain the relationship among all these traits. Such a structure—what we will here call an *anatomy*—might help us to understand how caring processes work within all helping relationships to make them more intentional and successful. For trained professionals and volunteers who serve a wide range of clients and patients, such an understanding is imperative because they know that caring involves more than doing good deeds for people. I make this point not to diminish the daily value of doing good things on behalf of others but to emphasize how particular helping relationships, those established by counselors, nurses, volunteers, and other helpers, demonstrate a specific kind of caring that has a high level of intentionality.

Professional helpers practice a form of caring that requires three fundamental conditions for this anatomy of intentional caring. As we might expect, these conditions are the bare skeleton of caring behavior but are nonetheless essential in understanding the function and distinction that care takes in intentional helping relationships. The three conditions are (1) a deep understanding of students, clients, and patients who receive our services; (2) a proficient and ethical use of specialized knowledge and skill; and (3) an orchestrated posture that exemplifies all the qualities and characteristics that define caring behaviors.

In this chapter, we will examine these three elements to learn how, individually and combined, they contribute to the anatomy of caring and successful helping relationships. Many of the ideas in this chapter are also discussed in other parts of this book. However, we explore them here as a means of bringing clarity to the process of intentional caring.

The first element is to develop an understanding and appreciation of how human perception influences every helping relationship. When we care about other people, we create the messages we send to illustrate our caring, and the person or persons for whom we intend those messages receive them. The receivers interpret these messages by assigning meaning according to their own perceptions of them within a particular time and space. Helpers who have a clear and accurate understanding of how human perception influences all relationships are better able to create the most caring and beneficial messages for their clients. At the same time, they are able to receive messages from their clients, interpret them accurately, and offer a facilitative response that moves the relationship in a positive direction.

The second essential condition is the way in which we combine meaningful characteristics into a particular philosophy of caring. This philosophy is explicitly tied to our perceptions of others and ourselves. Three specific characteristics seem especially valuable: our capacity to maintain trustworthy relationships, our flexibility in working with and caring for clients, and the consistency with which we demonstrate positive regard for all the people we serve. In Chapter 4, we will consider this element in greater detail when we learn about the encouraging stance of an intentional helper.

The third component in the anatomy of caring is appropriate use of expert knowledge and skill. As mentioned in Chapter 2, intentional helpers have the potential to do great good with those who confide in them. Proper care requires adequate knowledge and competent skill combined with a high level of respect and regard for each client, all while moving the helping relationship toward beneficial goals.

THE POWER AND CHALLENGE OF HUMAN PERCEPTION

Every time we establish a helping relationship, our interactions with students, clients, and patients are influenced by the complex dynamics of perception—theirs and ours. As helpers, we bring our own unique perceptions to every relationship. Likewise, each client brings a singular view of life, his or her private world, and relationships with other people.

Perception is a powerful process because, once we have assigned particular meaning to certain events, we embrace that interpretation fervently, allowing it to

Reflection

> Think of a time you attempted to care for someone who rejected your overtures. As you reflect on this experience, identify perceptions that might have interfered with the help you were trying to give. Is there anything you would do differently today?

become part of our being. Everything we do, every thought we have, and every experience we encounter are processed through our perceptual channels; and this is true for our clients as well. Such perceptions become what cognitive theorists (Salkovskis, 1996) call *core beliefs,* which "consist of the most sensitive component of the self-concept" (Beck, 1996, p. 14). Usually, these core beliefs are balanced by compensatory rules. For example, "if I consistently show affection, I will be loved." In addition, some cognitive theorists say that these core beliefs create schemas consisting of organized elements of past events, experiences, and reactions that form a unwavering conclusion that guides future perceptions and interpretations (McGinn & Young, 1996). The theory that schemas "are highly independent, and probably are hierarchically arranged" (Meichenbaum, 1985) is similar to Purkey's (1970, 1978) assumption about the self-concept as an organized construct "characterized by harmony and orderliness" (Purkey, 1970, p. 7).

One basic assumption of cognitive theory is that cognitive change is central to the human change process. "Behavioral and emotional improvement is possible only if the mediating cognitive products, processes, and structures change" (Clark & Steer, 1996, p. 77). Because perceptions are so powerful, people are reluctant to change them; this is one of the basic challenges that helpers and clients face when trying to make decisions or alter behaviors to bring about life changes. Each participant in a helping relationship, helper and helpee alike, resists giving up certain perceptions because these beliefs and values are used over a lifetime to define who we are. If we change them, we risk changing ourselves, which can be a frightening and threatening prospect.

Perceptions are also challenging because they embrace all our unique traits and characteristics. No two individuals have an identical perception of the same event. Clark and Steer (1996) noted, "All perception, learning, and knowing are products of an information-processing system that actively selects, filters, and interprets environmental and other sensory stimuli that impinge on the individual" (p. 76). This can be particularly challenging to helpers who work with groups of clients. For example, marriage counselors are often faced with couples who have opposing views of the reasons for their marital discord. The husband may believe that the wife is too demanding, while she maintains that he does not do his fair share to keep the relationship healthy. Understanding how these different perceptions are contributing to the problem and interpreting them accurately for the couple is one of the steps the marriage counselor might take toward resolution.

Perception and Caring

We shape our worlds on the basis of the experiences we perceive. The events around us, the actions we choose in response to these events, and the behaviors other people choose in relating to us have meaning because we define and interpret these situations according our own perceptual frame of reference. The way in which we define and interpret all these happenings is our *reality* (Clark & Steer, 1996). So no matter how often or how strongly other people question these beliefs, we adhere to them with great passion because they define who we are. For example, if a young student believes fervently that he is not very smart, simply having teachers, counselors, and others tell him that his belief is untrue will be insufficient to bring about a change in perception. To alter this or other "realities" that the student might have about his competency as a pupil, they might have to introduce him to many new events and experiences that contradict his old views. Such repeated exposure would be contrary to his long-held beliefs, causing him to question what he formerly believed to be true. Perhaps he would start realizing success in his schoolwork rather than repeated failure. Being successful in some of his schoolwork could help to alter a belief that he can't do the work.

All clients who seek our assistance have unique and powerful perceptions about themselves and their world. Their life experiences have only the meaning that they give to them. Consequently, the interpretations that other people might give to these same events only have value to the degree that they agree with a client's point of view. As we encourage clients to examine their beliefs and behaviors, the most critical element to understand at the start of every helping relationship is the perceptual world each client has created in her or his own mind—the personal meaning each gives to her or his private world. This understanding cannot be underestimated. As Combs and Gonzalez (1994) noted, "the moment we understand other people in terms of personal meaning, a great deal that was formerly puzzling or inexplicable becomes meaningful and reasonable" (p. 72).

Each of us has unfulfilled goals, dreams, and desires. Such aspirations are frequently blocked because of our self-beliefs about inadequacies, weaknesses, or fears that would make it virtually impossible to accomplish them. For example, someone might have the desire to hang-glide but has never attempted—could never try it—because of a fear of height. If one wants to hang-glide bad enough, the fear of height must be altered: that reality has to change. If you really want to do what you wrote in the reflection below, what beliefs will you have to change to make it happen?

As we examine our self-beliefs more closely, we might discover some past perceptions that once inhibited our development but now no longer influence us. Learning about the events and processes that helped us to alter these former beliefs can lead us to deeper self-understanding and perhaps to altering other unwanted perceptions. More important, it might enable us to appreciate how difficult it can be for students, clients, and patients to achieve similar goals in their lives.

Reflection

To test the veracity of the power of perception, you might examine some self-beliefs that are difficult for you to alter. Ask yourself the following question, and fill in the blank to complete the inquiry:

"What do I believe about myself that prevents me from _____?"

We can also understand the power of human perception by thinking about the beliefs we have retained about ourselves since childhood. For most of us, the strongest beliefs that we created during childhood remain into our adult years. Chores that we hate to do, foods we like and dislike, social events we enjoy or find discomforting, and a multitude of other experiences hold the same meaning today as they did when we were younger. The longevity of these beliefs is evidence of their powerful influence on our development as individuals.

Because of the power that perceptions lend to our development, the care that we give in helping clients and patients examine their beliefs plays a vital role in every helping relationship. Counselors, nurses, and other helpers who understand this role are better able to balance the care they give with the knowledge and skill required in their respective professions. In contrast, people who attempt to help others by telling them the "right way" to do things, how to "see things" differently, or not to "feel the way" they do will surely struggle to be successful. This is particularly true when caregivers are trying to help people overcome strong fears that are inhibiting their development.

All people have fears and anxieties of one form or another. At times, our fears are based on logical conclusions and are therefore understandable. For example, in the midst of a terrifying hurricane, most of us would experience some level of trepidation. Other times, our fears may be irrational, even to us. We know they exist because we experience them first hand, but we do not fully understand why we have them. Such fears confuse and frustrate us and the people with whom we associate. They are confusing because we do not know how we acquired them or where they came from, and they are frustrating because we do not know how to get rid of them. For example, a generalized fear of dogs could be incapacitating to a person who likes to walk around the neighborhood. Perceptions that feed our irrational fears are powerful because they strap us to inhibitions that obstruct healthy development.

Successful helpers who assist people with these types of fears do so with utmost care and regard for each person's private world. Demonstrating such care means first understanding that the fear, which seems to be a controlling behavior, is a manifestation of underlying perceptions, a person's inner beliefs, that hold the power and define his or her anxieties.

Many students, clients, and patients come for assistance because they think they have lost control of their lives. Marriage partners who are divorcing, workers who have lost jobs, students who are failing in school, parents who feel helpless in dealing with their adolescents, and people who are losing loved ones due to terminal illness are just a few examples of situations that cause people to think they are losing or have lost control. In many cases, these stressful events lead to disabling beliefs, fed by mistaken or misguided perceptions that allow clients and patients to fear the worst for themselves. By showing appropriate care, we accept all these perceptions and encourage clients to examine them thoroughly before determining what they want to do about them.

Sometimes we help clients discover powerful perceptions they can use to overcome obstacles and accomplish goals that might once have seemed unimaginable. Again, this can only be done when we create an appropriate and caring relationship. For example, consider the relationship between a coach and an athlete. Successful coaches are able to help athletes bring forth talents and abilities they might not fully realize on their own. Several factors enable this special relationship between coaches and players. First, coaches and athletes must have mutual respect. Even when coaches push their athletes hard to achieve better performance, ideally they do so out of respect for each athlete's unique talents and capabilities. At the same time, the athletes accept the instruction because they have high regard for the coach's knowledge and expertise in the sport. Without such admiration, few players would follow a coach's guidance.

Another factor related to mutual respect and high regard is a coach's concern for each athlete's welfare. Although athletic training is often rigorous and takes some bodily risk, no successful coach jeopardizes an athlete's future by asking players to take unwarranted risks or to put themselves in harm's way.

In the same way, we, as caring helpers, sometimes invite clients to search deep within themselves and find courage that they might not think they had. As noted, changing strongly held beliefs is not easy, so clients need our encouragement. Such encouragement may come in the form of challenging existing perceptions and asking students, clients, and patients to question the veracity of their own beliefs, some of which they fervently embrace despite knowing how these perceptions cause problems. When we offer help in such dramatic form, it is essential that we provide all the necessary safeguards to ensure a trusting relationship, one in which the client is properly protected and where we closely monitor progress.

Perception and the Challenge of Helping

Although cognitive theorists and others have developed models and posited assumptions to help us understand perceptual phenomena, people can nevertheless observe the same event and draw opposing conclusions. We witness this mystery every day. Ask classroom teachers about the lessons they have taught, and they will report a variety of student understandings about their instruction. The students have the same teacher, use the same instructional materials, hear the same lesson during the same time period, but come to different conclusions about what is important and what they have learned.

Another common example is when traffic police investigate an accident by interviewing eyewitnesses. Without fail, witnesses will recall contradictory details about the mishap they have just seen. One account reports the car was speeding, while a second

Reflection

Knowing your own level of tolerance for risk taking might heighten your appreciation of your clients' apprehensions. What level of risk are you willing to take to make changes in your life?

says it was blocking traffic. Another claims the driver tried to avoid hitting the other car, but a bystander insists, "He lost control and swerved into the oncoming vehicle."

Consider when counselors or therapists attempt to mediate differences with couples or groups. The client who perceives his own behaviors as supportive and encouraging may be accused by his partner of being controlling and domineering. The challenge for the therapist is to help each of them understand how their various perceptions have developed and why each viewpoint is accurate for each partner.

What all these observations tell us is that our perceptions are formed in unique and mysterious ways. Each of us processes new experiences through a perceptual passageway comprised of past events and perceptions we have retained as part of our self-concept. Over time, we have constructed these perceptions into a belief system that defines ourselves and the world in which we live. As such, when we perceive new events and experiences, old conclusions and interpretations that are part of our being color our views. This process of coloration explains, in part, some of the mystery about human perception. Yet this part of human functioning remains largely unknown to scientists and practitioners. Counselors and other helpers who embrace the theory of perceptual psychology believe that the sum of our perceptions creates a special view of life, the world around us, and our place in it. It is from this perceptual framework that clients and helpers make decisions and choose behaviors to satisfy life's needs. Cognition mediates affect and behavior. This situation does not equate to a causal relationship between perceptions and behavior; rather, "cognition, emotion, and behavior are reciprocally determining and interactive constructs in the process (Clark and Steer, 1996, p. 77).

As helpers, we take into account the unique processes that our clients use to form conclusions about who they are and what the future might hold for them. To ignore this important element might inhibit growth in our helping relationships and could negatively influence how we ultimately use our knowledge and skill.

A PHILOSOPHY OF HELPING

Understanding and appreciating the power and challenge of human perceptions leads us to the next element in the anatomy of caring: establishing a healthy philosophy on which to base appropriate use of our knowledge and skill. The powerful perceptions that define who we are as helpers establish a philosophy that is the basis of our caring and helping. We might not fully comprehend this philosophy and struggle to articulate it to others; nevertheless, it exists as a foundation of our selves as helpers. In Chapter 4, we will explore this foundation in greater depth, but here we want to introduce three elements fundamental to the anatomy of caring: trustworthiness, flexibility, and respectfulness.

Being Trustworthy

Trust is a condition that all genuine helpers attempt to create. We convey to our clients how important it is for them to share thoughts, feelings, and other facts about themselves and to trust us to use this information respectfully. Occasionally, however, helpers express this expectation without reciprocating. For example, a mental health counselor might expect clients to divulge their innermost thoughts and feelings readily, but the counselor may not show that she is willing to self-disclose similar experiences and emotions to facilitate the helping relationship. Similarly, we ask our clients and patients to behave in a trustful manner, yet we occasionally fail to follow through on commitments we have made to them. For example, a nurse expects a patient to follow instructions in taking prescribed medicines; but if the patient has asked for reminders and the nurse frequently forgets to give the necessary prompts, the trust between them is fragile at best.

In caring relationships, trust is built by the way in which helpers behave as well as how clients perceive the help they are given. Thus, trust is a two-way proposition. Moreover, it does not develop simply because we expect it. We must demonstrate consistently and dependably to our clients and patients that we are trustworthy professionals and volunteers. This means they must perceive us as being genuine with the care we give them. It also means that they trust us to act responsibly, perform our services competently, and follow through on our promises and commitments.

When we establish relationships by expecting clients or patients to trust us completely without having faith that they want to achieve, make appropriate decisions, and lead healthier lives, a trusting partnership cannot fully develop. To complete a trustworthy relationship, we allow our clients and patients to take responsibility for their welfare and resist unreasonable dependency they might have on us. This aspect of being trustworthy is not as easy as it sounds. Sometimes we are reluctant to allow our clients freedom to make certain decisions because we are apprehensive about which choices they might make. It is imperative that clients and patients take responsibility for their lives. Our role as caring helpers is to minimize the risks involved, be certain our clients have the developmental capacity, set up safety nets in case they fall, and make ourselves available when they need us. Ultimately, we have faith that our clients and patients will take responsible action. Without faith in their potential to make appropriate personal and social decisions and take charge of their lives, we cannot establish fully trustful and caring relationships.

Maintaining Flexibility

Highly skilled and technical helpers risk becoming so precise with their strategies that they abandon all hope of flexibility with patients and clients. This is analogous to

Reflection

Trust has always been listed as one of the goals that helpers must attain in their helping relationships. Taking a fresher perspective, we might say that helpers should demonstrate trustful behaviors early in the helping process rather than set trust as a goal of the relationship. If trust is the product of earlier events, how do you see yourself establishing trust with distrustful clients?

speeding straight ahead with blinders on rather than maintaining a wide, peripheral vision. Precision in helping relationships has its place, particularly in critical situations such as medical emergencies. Nevertheless, as noted in Chapter 2, when we consistently adhere to a singular point of view, a solitary strategy, or a lone approach to helping, regardless of the situation, we put at risk all the essential elements of caring.

At the same time, being flexible does not mean being overly permissive, although in some therapeutic relationships a degree of permissiveness might be appropriate. Flexibility does not mean letting clients and patients do whatever they want. If we allow any kind of behavior to define our helping relationships, we risk the interpretation that "anything goes." Consequently, we put ourselves at the opposite end of the helping spectrum. Rather than being rigid and narrow-minded, we become chaotic and uncommitted. Furthermore, clients might conclude that our willingness to accept any type of behavior indicates that we do not genuinely care about them. In their eyes, we might simply be going through the motions of helping. Therefore, as caring helpers, we are sometimes obliged to oppose our client's wishes and stand fast. C. Gilbert Wrenn (1996) explained, "Caring is saying 'no' firmly at times, but with a willingness to give reasons" (p. 80). For example, when a patient asks a nurse to increase pain medication over the prescribed limit or a client invites a therapist to attend a social function together, the response must be no. In these and similar instances, reasonable firmness and opposition are the caring stances to take. Yet, of course, in the previous example, a compassionate nurse follows up on the patient's request by consulting with medical staff to ensure that they have prescribed an appropriate dosage of medication to relieve the pain. Similarly, a therapist might attend the social function separately to show appropriate support for the client, thereby enhancing trust in their relationship.

Today the varied helping professions exist in a world of managed care and adherence to specific diagnoses. Does such a climate add to or detract from patient and client care? Such inflexibility is analogous to our educational system's obsession with measuring student achievement through excessive testing programs and rigid standards for all students regardless of their developmental strengths and weaknesses.

By flexibility, we mean keeping our options open and encouraging our students, clients, and patients to do the same. We listen carefully while resisting the urge to impose our will, always mindful of the welfare and best interest of our clients. This philosophy is not contrary to the structure necessary in helping relationships. An appropriate and healthy degree of flexibility enables us to define the structural nature, purpose, and goals of our helping relationships within a context of caring. In this way, we demonstrate appropriate regard for both the helping process and our clients.

Demonstrating Positive Regard

An additional element in the anatomy of caring is how we show respect and positive regard to our clients. Carl Rogers and many other theorists have assigned great importance to this element in the helping process. Here, we consider what it means in terms of caring for others.

Being respectful of others is an important characteristic in all human relationships. In our helping relationships, however, the demonstration of respect and positive regard takes on a particular and special meaning that denotes action. This means that being respectful in a helping relationship is more than simply *not* showing disrespect. It is the active display of genuine regard, admiration, affection, and concern for our clients and patients. Relationships that do not consist of these qualities, actively demonstrated, most likely will not reach a very high level of intentional helping. This is not to say that such relationships are unhelpful because they probably are. They just do not exhibit a degree of caring that defines optimal helping.

Consider a social worker who is assisting a family with financial aid. He asks the family for the necessary information, stoically showing little emotion and not demonstrating genuine acceptance of the family members. He proceeds to complete the proper forms and files them in a timely manner so the family qualifies for assistance. In essence, the social worker did the job and thus was "helpful." But what could he have done to bring the relationship to a higher level of functioning? How could he have helped the family members feel significant and worthwhile?

Sometimes simply doing what is expected is insufficient. By failing to demonstrate positive regard and respect to our clients, we disenfranchise them despite the helpful tasks we might complete on their behalf. Once an African American colleague and I went out for lunch and decided to stop by a shopping mall for an ice-cream cone. We walked up to the counter and, as we looked over the choices, drifted to opposite ends of the display. When I made my selection, I said to the waitress, "I'm paying for my friend's ice cream also." She immediately assumed that I meant a white man, like me, who was now standing between my friend and myself at the counter. When I corrected her and pointed to my colleague at the end of the display, she said, "Oh, I didn't think that could be your friend." She served us our ice cream, but the thoughtless comment showed a clear lack of regard. I still recall my colleague's response as we walked away. He shook his head and said, "Yeah, how could she possibly think *we* were friends!"

Respectfulness and positive regard complete a philosophy of helping and, in combination with all the perceptions we interpret, allow us to choose appropriate behaviors to use our knowledge and skill. Having a healthy philosophy of helping is beneficial to others when we demonstrate competent knowledge and skill within caring relationships.

USING KNOWLEDGE AND SKILL APPROPRIATELY

By using knowledge and skill appropriately, we exemplify traits and characteristics that have historically identified effective helpers (Combs & Gonzalez, 1994). Researchers have compiled numerous studies over the past several decades to demonstrate that acceptance of clients' perceptions contributes to the success of helping relationships. At the same time, research shows that a focus on how the helper perceives the client, him or herself, and others seems to influence the quality of help given. As Combs and Gonzalez (1994) have summarized, "A number of research studies have demonstrated that clear differences between good and poor practitioners in the helping professions are found when attention is focused on the perceptual organization or belief systems of the helper" (p. 19). Patterson and Hidore (1997) echoed this finding in their assessment of effective therapeutic conditions. Surveying studies ranging from Carl Rogers's work in the 1950s to the review of Beutler and colleagues in 1994, they concluded that few things are as certain as the consistent evidence supporting the "necessity if not sufficiency of the therapist conditions of accurate empathy, respect, or warmth, and therapeutic genuineness" (Patterson, 1984, p. 437).

Combs and Gonzalez (1994) have presented five areas of helper beliefs and perceptual functioning that research shows are related to effective helping: the expression of empathy and sensitivity, positive versus negative views about other people and oneself, the underlying purpose of helping, and the authenticity with which helping methods are practiced. Each of these areas influences how and why professional and volunteer helpers express their care for students, clients, and patients. As we learned in Chapter 1, they are also essential elements in understanding what it means to care.

Beliefs and Caring

By using our knowledge and skill appropriately, we dependably express our sensitivity toward the people we aim to help. As noted, this means listening with genuine care and accepting their perceptions of the situation under consideration. This is the fundamental starting point for all successful helping relationships. The assistance we attempt to give others will be successful to the degree that we embrace who these people are and what they are experiencing as viewed from their unique perspective. In this regard, Wrenn (1996) posited, "Caring is reinforcing the other person's concept of himself/herself as a worthwhile person" (p. 80). Prematurely sharing our views or asking clients to see things in a different way will not facilitate the relationships we establish. In fact, such autocratic behavior might push clients away and thwart our ability to be helpful.

Positive views of people have been found to be strong correlates to effective helping. What helpers generally believe about their clients and patients are conveyed as expectations in the helping relationship. The teacher who greets a new student with "It's great to have you in class, I have heard many good things about you!" sets a positive tone to begin the school year. Likewise, the juvenile court counselor who starts the first session by expressing optimism that the young detainee can overcome past difficulties initiates the relationship on a hopeful note.

Positive self-views are also powerful factors for helpers. As we learned in Chapter 1, factors that sometimes underlie a person's motivation to help might not always emanate from a psychologically healthy outlook. On occasion, we see people take helping roles to satisfy their own basic and sometimes insidious needs. Such motivations are often the consequence of negative self-images—feelings of inferiority that block individuals from forming truly caring relationships.

Psychological research collected over several decades tells us that what we believe about ourselves is the single most important factor for behaving the way we do (Bandura, 1994; Purkey, 2000; Schunk & Zimmerman, 1994). Therefore, positive views of ourselves will contribute to the caring relationships we form, while negative views will inhibit our relations with others. Several research studies verify that effective helpers see themselves in positive ways (Combs & Gonzalez, 1994). They are confident, capable, accepted, and wanted by others. All these qualities are essential because they allow us to set a firm foundation of principles by which we help others. Without such principles—what we call in Chapter 4 an *encouraging stance*—we cannot possibly have the courage and the psychological strength to care deeply and dependably for people from diverse backgrounds who are facing various life struggles.

Combs and Gonzalez (1994) noted that studies of helper purposes "clearly distinguish between good and poor helpers" (p. 25). Overall, effective helpers tend to view their relationships with clients and patients as ways of freeing individuals to become more than they are rather than situations in which the helper prescribes what people need to perform or conform to the norm. Facilitative helpers look for broad, encompassing purposes, while those who seek more control in their relationships tend to focus on narrow, precise goals.

Of course, in some caring relationships, such as nursing, precision is an important quality that cannot be diminished. The wrong dose of medication or a careless decision to remove an intravenous tube might be lethal. The important point is that even in relationships that demand short-term, precise goals and controlled behavior, the helper maintains a broader focus on the health and well-being of clients and patients. This global perspective distinguishes the strict technician from the truly caring helper.

Another aspect that interacts with our beliefs and how we care for others is our authenticity. The ways that we choose to help others are defined by the methods, techniques, and processes learned in preparing for our professional and volunteer roles. In all helping professions, there are numerous ways to assist others, and sometimes these are highly technical processes that require extensive training, such as biofeedback used by behavioral therapists or hypnotism used in hypnotherapy. Other methods may result from choices we make as helpers among various theories of practice, such as when a counselor chooses between a phenomenological approach and a cognitive behavioral strategy. What seems to be most important in establishing caring relationships is not the approach, method, or technique but the authenticity with which we apply our knowledge and skills (Sexton, 1999). By authenticity, we mean both the genuineness with which we use any particular methods (how open are we with the client, and how sensitive are we about the client's feelings about these methods?) and the flawlessness by which we apply our skills (how proficient are we?).

Caring helpers do not use methods that cannot be fully explained to their clients and patients. They are open about the processes they use, and they involve clients, as appropriate, in all decisions about applied approaches and techniques. This stance creates an egalitarian relationship, an authentic acceptance of the client or patient. At the same time, caring helpers know what methods show promise in particular situations, and they are proficient in using specific techniques suggested to clients. Such authenticity is paramount to ensuring ethical practice in all helping relationships.

Culture and Caring

All the elements mentioned in this chapter that contribute to our belief system as helpers accept people who might have different views than our own. Culture, background, and heritage must also interact with our desire and ability to care and be intentionally helpful.

The world in which we function as helpers is rapidly changing, particularly with regard to the interactions among people of diverse cultures and backgrounds. In the United States, increased cultural diversity is apparent in almost every town, city, and region of the country. Even in rural towns, where people have historically lived, grown, and remained over a lifetime, the influx of people from different regions and countries has forced issues of diversity. As I write this book, I am living in North Carolina, a beautiful state rich with heritage, culture, and tradition. Over the years, I have traveled through many villages that are picturesque reflections of yesterday. People in these communities know each other, go to the same churches, talk in similar ways, and to a visitor present a homogenous image of small-town America.

Today, in many of these towns, some visitors have stayed, and their presence has altered the visible homogeneity that once existed. For example, in many rural areas of North Carolina, people of Latino origin have immigrated to find work on tobacco farms, in cotton fields, in the building trades, and in other types of employment. In many instances, these people have come to the state from Mexico. But for many rural townspeople, Mexico is not just "south of the border." It is much more foreign than that. "South of the border" to many North Carolinians means South Carolina! Nevertheless, in some of these instances, townspeople have altered their perceptions as a result of this Mexican influence.

For helpers, understanding the impact that people of diverse cultures have on a community is important to providing appropriate care. At the same time, the multicultural movement emphasizes the value of recognizing the beliefs and traits that people share (Patterson & Hidore, 1997). As helping professions in the United States have incorporated knowledge and skills to better assist people from diverse backgrounds, our understanding of multiculturalism as a concept has become more inclusive. In the early years of the multicultural movement, we focused on minority groups such as Asian Americans, African Americans, Latinos, and others. Today, the movement embraces a much broader focus, including gender issues, sexual orientation, racial makeup, socioeconomic levels, age factors, and other cultural dimensions.

Throughout the multicultural movement (which began roughly 30 years ago), helpers such as counselors, therapists, and social workers have tried to learn skills and behaviors to use, or not to use, with particular groups. Inherent in this philosophical trend has been the belief that different groups need different approaches to helping. This has been particularly emphasized in the literature of the counseling professions, where many authors have proclaimed that the popular theories of counseling are based essentially on a white, European perspective. The conclusion drawn by many authorities is that such a narrow basis is inappropriate for use with the broad range of cultural groups with whom counselors work.

Much of the multicultural counseling literature continues to focus how to better serve clients of diverse cultures. Researchers initially tried to define specific skills required by different populations and identify the knowledge base needed to help particular groups of clients. As the number of identified cultures, subgroups, and diverse populations multiplied, however, the complexity of this challenge became increasingly more apparent. In response to this dilemma, Patterson and Hidore (1997) have suggested that we revisit basic therapeutic qualities to find universal characteristics essential to all helping relationships.

Although research has yet to show us which specific skills are more effective or what essential knowledge is imperative when helping particular cultural groups, the fundamental elements of caring seem to cross all societies and subgroups. This means that, as intentional helpers, we recognize and understand differences that exist between our clients and us. Equally important, however, we focus on common humane elements that enable us to connect and relate to our fellow human beings (Vontress, 1988). Our willingness to listen genuinely; the degree to which we empathize with understanding; and our acceptance of people who appear different from us culturally, socially, or in some other fashion are universal characteristics of helping and demonstrating care for others. All the knowledge and skill we use as helpers are reflections of our philosophy of caring, and this belief system is closely tied to our perceptions. Combined, these three components and their individual characteristics form an anatomy of caring.

Figure 3.1 depicts the main elements of this anatomy, showing how perception forms a foundation on which our philosophy is built and that appropriate use of knowledge and skill is predicated on a healthy philosophy. As such, our perceptions and those of our students, clients, and patients help to define our philosophy of helping and set the parameters for appropriate use of our knowledge and skill. This is the structure that enables us to care about, for, and with other people. In a sense, it illustrates metaphorically the heart of helping. When we do not follow these principles, we fall prey to the human weakness of not caring.

Reflection

What cultural experiences have been most influential in your development as a person and a professional helper? How do these experiences affect your work with clients?

FIGURE 3.1 *Caring: The heart of helping*

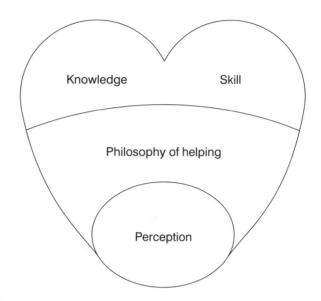

NOT CARING

If we can illustrate a structure for intentional caring, such as the anatomy presented in this chapter, it follows that there might also be a structure for not caring. By *not caring,* I mean the times when we behave with malice as well as when we are noncommittal or apathetic toward people who seek our assistance.

There are countless reasons why we allow ourselves to falter in attempts to help other people. Sometimes daily stress and fatigue contribute to unhelpful attitudes. At other times the resistance or stubbornness of clients influences our negative feelings and subsequently careless or thoughtless behaviors. Understanding the potential dichotomy for caring and uncaring behavior helps us not only become more aware of when we exhibit such behaviors but also understand with greater empathy why some clients and patients repeatedly tell us they "don't care."

Underlying a structure for perpetually not caring are negative perceptions of self and others, which are the foundation of a belief system that perpetuates hostile, argumentative, neglectful, wasteful, and other forms of uncaring behavior. Such a belief system may lead to inappropriate use of knowledge and skills and begin a cycle of reinforcing negative perceptions on which the belief system rests. For healthy professional and volunteer helpers, the occasional slip into an uncaring mode of behavior is, as we have emphasized, temporary, usually brought on by brief careless actions, often unintended. Sometimes marked by absentmindedness, distraction, or disengagement, these short-lived regressions are usually correctable. We ask forgiveness from those offended and move forward with our relationships. But for people who live in a constant state of not caring, the challenge to make healthy life choices and changes is much greater.

As helpers, our task is to use all the intentional qualities presented in this book to show clients that, even though they do not care, we do. Many years ago, I worked as an elementary school counselor. If you have worked with young children, you know that, when frustrated, they often say, "I don't care." When I heard students say this to teachers, I usually heard teachers snap, "Well, if you know what is good for you, you'll start caring." Rarely, however, did I notice that this response facilitated constructive change in the relationship or in the child's disposition.

Two responses that I found helpful in working with children who appeared to have given up on themselves illustrate the acceptance and encouragement essential to forming successful helping relationships. The first was to accept that the children didn't care at the moment and ask if it was all right that I cared about them. I never had a child who refused my desire to care. When we are frustrated and despondent, having another human being express genuine concern can be a soothing remedy.

The second useful response was to encourage children to talk about things that they *did* care about. In part, this response helped young clients focus on an agenda they wanted to work on. It also moved the relationship toward positive issues that they subsequently used to learn how to handle identified concerns and problems. Together, these two responses moved the helping relationship toward goals that children felt were most important to them. This is key to any helpful relationship: identifying a constructive purpose that the client cares about.

Reflection

When you feel yourself slipping into an apathetic or not caring mode, or when you feel like throwing up your hands in resignation because a client continues to falter, what strategies can you use to correct such situations?

In this chapter, we have considered many aspects that relate to our ability to demonstrate appropriate care. These include an understanding of human perception and the challenge it presents in all helping relationships. We have also explored the importance of developing a philosophy of caring that includes being trustworthy, maintaining flexibility, and demonstrating positive regard toward others. Finally, this chapter has emphasized within an anatomy of caring the appropriate use of knowledge and skill with all clients regardless of cultural differences. Through our understanding, beliefs, and appropriate use of skill and knowledge, we are able to help students, patients, and clients choose suitable goals.

Helping clients identify clear purposes and useful goals, as emphasized throughout this book, takes a certain degree of intention on our part. It also takes a willingness to create positive messages that have a chance of being accepted by students, clients, and patients. In Chapter 4, we will examine one model of creating caring messages.

4

Creating Caring Messages

We are surrounded by invitations, from formal requests to informal urgings, to trust, buy, eat more, eat less, do this, do that, and to develop spiritually, socially, intellectually, and physically.

William Watson Purkey
Inviting School Success, 1978, p. 2

Ever since humankind first began attending to relationships among people, we have searched for models of communication to explain our limitless interactions and associations. In the helping professions, we have given much effort to finding efficacious approaches that facilitate human relationships, problem solving, conflict resolution, marital enrichment, career decision making, and countless other interactions influencing people's lives. At last count, several hundred approaches have been reported in the literature, although many fewer have been rigorously tested and proven to be viable models of helping. Still, a conceptual structure for processing one's thoughts and behaviors may be useful, regardless of the type of helping relationship being established.

In this chapter, we examine one such structure for communicating with others. It is a model adapted from *Invitational Counseling* developed by William Purkey and myself (Purkey & Schmidt, 1996), an approach that embraces the basic tenets of perceptual psychology and self-concept theory. Like other communication models promoted by the helping professions, invitational counseling can enable people to reach out to others. If not used in an empathic, ethical, and appropriate manner, however, it may create harmful encounters that reflect the darker side of human intentionality (Purkey & Schmidt, 1996).

The invitational theory of communication is useful in helping relationships because its theoretical base—self-concept theory and perceptual psychology—includes assumptions that underlie all caring relationships. The beliefs that people hold about themselves and the conclusions they draw about others and the world around them help establish a basis for choosing from a wide range of caring and uncaring behaviors. That basis, as we have learned in this book, is their intentionality. To ensure that the invitational model is applied carefully, we first create a stance that truly encourages everyone involved in the process to be equally vested and involved in the helping relationship, with the ultimate goal being the development of each person's full potential.

AN ENCOURAGING STANCE

Every helping relationship begins with certain fundamental beliefs—a philosophy, if you will—about ourselves and the people we attempt to help. These beliefs form the core value system of our intentionality and therefore guide us in a particular direction and with an underlying purpose. As noted in previous chapters, caring relationships maintain the most positive direction and beneficial purpose for everyone involved, and they require consistency and dependability. These goals may seem overly idealistic, particularly given the range of human conditions, but it is imperative that intentional helpers maintain their belief of doing ultimate good. To think otherwise weakens our resolve, which even during challenging times must be measured against the highest possible standard. It is easy to help when all conditions are favorable and people are receptive to our assistance. In other words, it is easier to remain positive when the sun is shining than when the rain is pouring down and your umbrella refuses to open! However, the hallmark of a truly caring relationship appears when, under frustrating circumstances and difficult conditions, we maintain a positive direction and persevere unselfishly.

In daily chronicles we find numerous examples of persistent and dependable helping. Relief workers and medical professionals extend themselves in extraordinary ways, assisting people on all sides during strife and disaster that tear apart families, leave people homeless, and create great human suffering. In the helping professions, counselors, social workers, and others persevere to help clients overcome illnesses, abuse, and other circumstances of hopelessness. Key to all these helping relationships are the ingredients that form each helper's belief system and ultimately create an encouraging stance from which that person acts.

Optimism

First among these ingredients is the belief that good things will happen—in other words, a generally optimistic view of the human condition and the potential of people

Reflection

What do you believe about the human condition and the potential of individuals to develop fully?

to work together. To create an encouraging stance, we must truly believe that the student, client, or patient can make positive changes in his or her life. Clearly, it would be counterproductive to attempt to assist another person if our underlying pessimistic attitude really says, "This isn't going to work." All successful helping relationships assume that everyone is capable of working toward common, beneficial goals.

Optimism acknowledges each person's ability to make things happen and embraces human potential. At the same time, however, it is tempered by realistic expectations, an understanding of the support and resources necessary to overcome obstacles and achieve objectives, and a willingness to learn about and meet future challenges. As Martin Seligman (1992) cautioned, optimism is not a panacea. Nevertheless, his studies show that an optimistic style does tend to thwart feelings of helplessness, while a pessimistic style fuels them. Helpers who take a reasonably optimistic stance are careful not to put their clients and others in unnecessary jeopardy. They are guided by a strong desire to reach for higher goals while keeping in mind their own level of competency and their clients' capabilities.

Optimistic helpers know their limitations and do not hesitate to seek guidance from professionals and others who have different skills and expertise. They also monitor their positive outlook to avoid conveying an unbridled idealism that is not particularly helpful and perhaps even harmful. For example, a counselor who encourages a client to adopt risky behaviors to overcome a phobia without establishing a sound schedule of desensitization or providing a safety net may put the client in harm's way. On the other hand, a counselor who continually encourages a client to take small steps while providing the necessary protection and support demonstrates appropriate faith in both the client and the helping process.

Another aspect of this optimistic posture is our own self-confidence as helpers. Believing that we can help is a necessary ingredient in establishing a successful relationship. When we do not believe in ourselves, our skills, and our knowledge, we may behave in ways that invite failure. For example, a social worker who doubts her ability to relate to families who are culturally different could unknowingly send messages that convey discomfort. In such instances, families will sense her uncertainty and might read her behavior as distrustful or repudiating. Their reading of the situation will likely raise their resistance and subsequently inhibit the overall helping relationship.

Studies have shown that self-confidence is a precursor to success in many different types of ventures. People who believe in themselves have the appearance of self-

Reflection

Conveying realistic optimism in helping relationships combines hopefulness with adequate knowledge and appropriate skill. How do you rate your overall optimism about life, other people's ideas, the clients with whom you work, and your ability to help them?

confidence, while those who lack self-assurance forecast their failures in the same way that an unskilled poker player reveals a hand without ever showing a card. Confident helpers convey their optimism to people who seek their assistance.

Respect

An optimistic posture leads to respect, which is also essential in helping relationships. As noted, when we are intentional with our direction and purpose, we have the power to be either a beneficial presence or a lethal force in the lives of those who seek our help. Respectfulness ensures the most constructive use of our helping skills. It requires an accurate understanding of who our clients are and where they are in their development or in the particular circumstance for which they are seeking our help. Without demonstrating respect for our clients and patients, we might not monitor the level of helpfulness of all our behaviors; and at the same time, our clients might not perceive our help as genuine.

By being consistently respectful, we illustrate the caring quality of our intentionality. In contrast, when we are unknowing or apathetic, we might behave in unintentional ways that clients view as disrespectful. Respectfulness enables us to establish high goals of self-responsibility and convey to others our appreciation for their responsible actions. People, however, define and perceive the word *respect* in various ways. As helpers, we need to understand what respect means to us so that we clearly and consistently demonstrate this quality for our clients.

Some professionals act as if they can demand respect from clients, but this is a fallacy. They might be able to demand *obedience*, but this does not necessarily equal respect. When people demand respect from others, their ultimatum is frequently not balanced by reciprocal and respectful behaviors. In these instances, people misunderstand the difference between respect and obedience. Respectful people, whether professionals or volunteers, understand this difference and, as a result, behave with genuine regard toward themselves and others. Usually, these people are respected and highly regarded in return.

Respectful behaviors encompass many of the qualities presented in this book. In helping relationships, we respect our students, clients, and patients by accepting who they are and treating them with utmost regard by recognizing the value and worth that each person brings to the relationship. Respect also means attending to

Reflection

Think about the signs posted around the building where you work. What do these signs convey in terms of respectfulness to the people who read these messages? How would you change problematic signs?

the perceptions that each client offers about the situation or concern at hand and accepting those views as integral to the person whom we are helping.

At the same time, respecting oneself is the first step to becoming a responsible helper. We define self-respect by the regard we have for ourselves, our recognition of our capabilities, and the intentionality with which we live our lives. Without respect for ourselves, we will probably not be able to behave in intentionally respectful ways toward others.

Sometimes helping relationships test the limits of our respect for those who seek our assistance. For example, clients who are under great stress, patients who suffer from terminal illnesses, and students who continually fail in school can bring out less than helpful behaviors from both clients and helpers. During these stressful situations, we may be tempted to resort to despair and resignation in response to our clients' behaviors and attitudes, but we cannot. *We must not.* At such challenging times, it is paramount that our most respectful behaviors persevere. By behaving in respectful ways at all times and under all circumstances, we accept people unconditionally and treat them with courtesy and civility.

Acceptance of others illustrates respect in two important ways. First, it demonstrates recognition of another person's value, regardless of his or her background and abilities. As Carl Rogers and other theorists have emphasized, this acceptance is unconditional. Consequently, we cannot truly care for, or care about, other people until we accept them in their totality. Although this goal sounds simple enough, reflective helpers understand that perceptions and prejudices sometimes interfere. Acquiring this understanding is the first step in negating our own biases, thereby becoming more effective helpers.

Our respect, acceptance, and ultimate responsibility as caring helpers are illustrated by how we receive responses from our students, clients, and patients and appreciate their individuality. We might not agree with everything they say or do, but we listen to their views and opinions with an open mind. We also understand that varied experience, heritage, and culture influence people's responses and reactions. Such qualities add richness and depth to our helping relationships.

A genuine demonstration of acceptance does not mean that we must be satisfied with all the unique attributes or agree with all the perspectives our clients bring to the helping relationship. On the contrary, accepting uniqueness is one step toward recognizing qualities with which we and our clients are dissatisfied and beginning to set goals to change them. In this way, we encourage people to accept responsibility for their unique qualities and attempt to change the ones they find undesirable.

Second, by accepting others we are accountable for our own actions while expecting them to be responsible for theirs. As caring helpers, we know the awesome responsibility of using our knowledge and skill to effect positive change. At the same time, we know that the skill and knowledge we possess are imperfect; sometimes, even with the best intentions, we make errors in judgment, assessment, and practice. Although we never excuse our mistakes, it is equally true that we do not accept blame for the irresponsible behaviors of people we are trying to help. Just as we are at the mercy of our human imperfections, our clients, patients, and counse-

Reflection

> Blame is an obstacle to accepting self-responsibility. As helpers, we consistently face the challenge of encouraging clients to take responsibility for their lives. We begin by helping them resist the temptation to blame others. How will you face the responsibility when your patients or clients do not progress as expected?

lees bring their own fears into each helping relationship and sometimes let these apprehensions lead to irresponsibility and blame.

In demonstrating a high level of direction and purpose, we consistently look for ways to increase our knowledge and skill to improve the quality and productivity of our helping relationships. Thus, we are careful not to remain stagnant. Doing so would contradict the respect we have for our profession and ourselves. It would also inhibit the development of trust, another characteristic of an encouraging stance.

Trust

Trust is essential to helping relationships and, as we learned in Chapter 3, vital to a caring philosophy. In most instances, trust develops in a helping relationship because the client or patient is comfortable with the helper. Such comfort exists because of the helper's faith in and respect for the client, which allow the person being helped to maintain her or his identity. According to Mayeroff (1971), trust is an appreciation of "the independent existence of the other, that the other is *other*" (p. 20). At the same time, the person being helped is encouraged by the realization that the helper "trusts me" (p. 20).

Sometimes in helping relationships, we refer to trust as a process of singular direction: the client must trust the helper. This is, at best, a limited view because trust is a two-directional quality. We trust ourselves as helpers because we have compassion and empathy for others, and we recognize the knowledge and skill we bring to particular helping relationships. As we extend our trust to others by demonstrating respect and acceptance, they, in turn, begin to develop faith in us. The helping relationship progresses as this trust becomes a more natural part of the process.

Self-knowledge enables us to depend on ourselves as reliable helpers with greater confidence. In this way, knowing more about our beliefs, values, and behaviors helps us become more self-assured. The more reliable, dependable, and confident we become, the more able we are to win the trust of others. For example, a nurse who cares for hospice patients will be more comfortable and confident in providing assistance as she or he becomes more aware of self-beliefs and values about death and dying.

As intentional helpers, we demonstrate trust by stating our expectations clearly. At the same time, we listen carefully to the hopes, dreams, and expectations of those whom we intend to help. Thus, trust is exemplified by a cooperative disposition that permits each person in the helping relationship to create a vision and work toward that ideal. If this disposition loses its cooperative tone, the relationship might falter. For example, counselors and other helpers may at times create goals that clients do not fully accept, or they might overly protect their clients from making mistakes. While these behaviors may be well intended, they violate the basic notions of trust in the client's ability. Caring helpers have the courage to allow their clients to make missteps in their journey toward a better life.

We do not mean to imply that helping is a permissive relationship that says anything the client wants is acceptable. On the contrary, a trustful helper knows when to set limits and expresses clear concern about the likely consequences of reckless and irresponsible actions. At the same time, helpers are willing to allow clients the freedom to choose, even at the risk of making nonlethal mistakes. When setbacks occur, they are ready to help clients learn from the experience. By demonstrating faith during trying circumstances, they express trust in their clients to overcome obstacles, meet challenges, and eventually succeed in their chosen endeavors.

The three ingredients of an encouraging stance—optimism, respect, and trust—include other related qualities such as hope, faith, acceptance, responsibility, and reliability. Together, all these qualities provide the substance of our intentionality as caring helpers. Without these positive ingredients, our direction and purpose might become less than helpful or uncaring. Figure 4.1 illustrates the relationship among all these qualities and helper intentionality, the core of which is caring.

A STRUCTURE FOR HELPFUL CARING

The qualities that influence our intentional helping and ultimate caring are challenging to maintain, even for the most devoted helpers. Being human, we are all susceptible to fatigue, stress, and other factors that detract from our desire to help others. In counseling, for example, the policies and procedures of an institution or system may become overbearing or overwhelming, thus forcing a counselor to place the student's, patient's, or client's needs behind the expectations of the school, hospital, or mental health system. At such times, a conceptual structure that guides us in processing our helping and caring relationships more efficiently might be a useful formula.

So far, we have learned that caring and helping consist of many qualities and ingredients that enable us to be successful as professional helpers. Because the process of helping requires selecting among these elements and behaviors, a con-

Reflection

Think of a time when you were not successful. What were the outcomes? Did you learn any positive lesson?

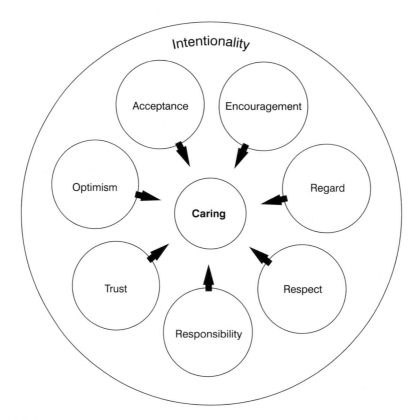

FIGURE 4.1 *Relationship of intentionality to aspects of caring*

ceptual structure may be useful in helping all parties reach mutually beneficial goals. The structure we consider here is not a step-by-step plan for caring but a series of observations about the actions that intentional helpers might choose. It is a guide for choosing behaviors and includes all the qualities and ingredients of caring we have examined thus far in this book. The first observation about essential actions is that we should have a desire to help.

Desiring

We demonstrate true concern and care for others only when we realize the desire to do so. In other words, we have to want to care. Wanting to care may be a simple notion, yet countless barriers and obstacles inhibit us from being optimal helpers. Most often the barriers we face are not physical or tangible ones so much as our own fears, doubts, and unwillingness to overcome prejudices and change attitudes. For example, a counselor who treats culturally different clients with a lack of respect demonstrates an inhibition about behaving appropriately and professionally. The counselor does not want to behave in an enlightened and caring manner.

Having the desire to help people and wanting to demonstrate our care for others do not exist in isolation. Our desire is influenced by fundamental beliefs about ourselves and people in general. These beliefs generate emotions, which in turn are guided by numerous factors. When we maintain a high degree of intentionality in the care we show to others, we are able to monitor our belief system and take charge of factors that influence all the helping relationships we establish. We understand that our desire to form beneficial relationships is affected by our belief system, our emotional well-being, and our physical strength and stamina. These factors are linked: when one of them is in jeopardy, it is likely to affect the others. For example, when we find ourselves becoming sluggish and unwilling to participate energetically and actively in helping others, we know that this physical condition might contaminate our thought processes. As a result, we may say or do things that are not in the best interest of the clients we intend to help. As caring helpers, we make every effort to avoid letting our physical condition have a negative influence on the help we provide. We also monitor behaviors that signal a need to change our routine. If we find ourselves repeatedly fatigued and excusing ourselves because we're too tired, we will examine our schedule to ensure sufficient breaks during the day or adequate sleep at night.

Counselors, nurses, and other helpers who examine their daily routine, monitor their diet, and maintain an exercise schedule do so to retain control of factors that enable them to be successful even during trying circumstances. Likewise, when they are under stress, they take charge of their schedule, make healthy changes, apply relaxation techniques, and, if needed, seek professional assistance to rejuvenate their emotional selves.

By examining and monitoring our desire to bring about changes in our own lives, we perform a rudimentary assessment of our willingness to help others. Perhaps people can maintain a desire to help and care for others even when they do not show equal concern for themselves, but we might question their credibility as genuine helpers. For example, can a person who continues to smoke cigarettes habitually win another's trust in designing a program to quit smoking?

Sometimes we desire to establish caring relationships but lack the preparation or knowledge requisite to being successful. Professional helpers understand that

Reflection

You can assess your level of wanting to help by examining specific instances of helping yourself. What aspects of your life have you wanted to change? It may be helpful to list the methods or activities you have initiated to bring about these changes. For example, if you have wanted to gain more knowledge about a particular helping skill, what have you done to acquire that level of expertise?

being prepared for particular relationships moves their willingness beyond the level of wanting to toward preparing for action.

Preparing

Intentionally caring helpers rarely step blindfolded or unprepared into relationships. Even in the most critical and urgent circumstances, we make every attempt to be ready for the twists and turns that helping relationships can take. Essential to this preparation is the knowledge we attain about particular human conditions and the skills we acquire to move each helping relationship toward a positive conclusion.

Professional helpers cannot possibly know everything about every situation, so our preparation must include a solid understanding of basic knowledge and competent use of helping skills. For example, social workers serve in a variety of agency and clinical settings, such as mental health services, schools, hospitals, and employee assistance programs. Each social worker comes to his or her specific work setting from undergraduate or graduate school preparation, having obtained basic knowledge about human development, social theory, approaches to helping, and other essential knowledge. Social workers also acquire a level of competency to use helping skills and methods of intervention and treatment appropriate for the professional setting in which they will practice. Similar illustrations could be given for counselors, nurses, family therapists, psychologists, and other helpers.

Consider the analogy of planning a party for friends. When we plan the party, we prepare our home and the celebration in ways that will please our guests and satisfy our desire to entertain. Purkey and Schmidt (1996) referred to this stage of readiness as "preparing the setting": we clean the house, plan what food to serve, select appropriate music to play or party activities to initiate, and design events to fit the nature and purpose of the celebration. The decisions we make in this planning process are based, in part, on what we know about the friends who are coming and the purpose of the party.

In much the same way, our helping relationships become successful when we prepare an appropriate setting, gain knowledge about the person or persons we are assisting, understand the purpose of the relationship, and convey this purpose clearly to those we are helping. Our ability to process these aspects of preparation is related to another quality of successful caregivers: their ability to read situations (Purkey & Schmidt, 1996).

Helping is a shared experience. As noted, it is not something we do to others but a process of caring about people, sharing our knowledge and skill, and capitalizing on each other's strengths to move the relationship forward. As intentional helpers, we understand the importance of learning about the people who seek assistance. Such knowledge enables us to read situations accurately. Without gaining knowledge and understanding the people we help, we risk misreading because, as Meier and Davis (1993) have noted, we make erroneous assumptions about our clients' feelings, thoughts, and behaviors.

If we return to the analogy of the party, we see how misreading situations can be problematic. Imagine that we have planned a wonderful surprise party for a friend who has confided that she is pregnant. Unfortunately, we have not taken time to learn about her feelings about surprise parties. More important, we do not know whether she has decided to tell people about the forthcoming baby. In fact, she has not. She wishes to be further along in the prenatal process before announcing her joy. The feelings she might experience when we unveil the surprise could span the range from anger to hurt. In any case, the risk we take in misreading situations like this one can be disastrous to our relationships with friends, colleagues, and loved ones.

Sometimes when we misread situations, we rely on our good intentions. In the party example, we might explain to our friend that we had her best interest in mind and thought she would be grateful to have friends celebrate her news. Again, we risk making many false assumptions when we read situations in this manner. As we have learned in this book, having good intentions might not always translate into caring relationships. Successful caregivers take time to learn about the people, situations, and circumstances involved in their helping relationships. By doing so, they increase their ability to read situations accurately and compassionately. At the same time, intentional helpers recognize that their ability to read every situation accurately is not absolute. On occasion, we will misread our clients and consequently make mistakes in the process of helping. What distinguishes us from consistently unintentional or misguided helpers is our willingness to admit the error. We explain and apologize to the client so that together we retrace steps that strengthen the relationship. Consequently, we become more effective helpers.

Ultimately, reading the situation means knowing what will work in a given relationship. Helpers who are skilled in this process expand their perceptual world to include limitless possibilities. They also become expert readers of human behavior. To achieve this level of competency, we learn about the people, situations, and circumstances involved in our helping relationships. At the same time, we avoid making assumptions simply because we have particular knowledge and skill.

We have seen that knowing what to do, preparing ourselves, and accurately reading situations provide the preliminary steps to creating caring messages. As helpers, we also realize that human interactions involve both sending and receiving messages. However, successful helping is more than just sending messages to those whom we assist. To be truly successful, we reach out to people, listening and

Reflection

Assess your ability to read situations accurately. Are you usually in tune with others or out of touch with what they mean by their words and actions? How do you verify your accuracy in reading situations?

responding appropriately to messages they send to us. What we say and do in this process defines the level of caring we demonstrate in every helping relationship.

Sending and Receiving

Purkey and Schmidt (1996) have referred to sending and receiving as the initiating and responding stage of invitational counseling. During this phase, helpers create opportunities for clients to explore issues, take stock of their situations, and make preliminary plans toward self-actualization. Nevertheless, when sending and receiving messages to help clients through this process of self-exploration, helpers should be cautious. Meier and Davis (1993) have suggested that we should avoid giving advice, solving problems prematurely, and relying on questions to facilitate the relationship. Instead, they emphasize listening carefully, attending to nonverbal messages, focusing on the client, being concrete, and summarizing to move the relationship forward. These attentive behaviors help us concentrate on the clients' agendas so that the messages we choose to send maintain a focus on them and their issues.

When we send messages in a helping relationship, we have an inherent responsibility. For this reason, we choose each message carefully, thus preparing ourselves and reading the situation. We also keep the client's best interest and welfare in mind. If we do, the messages we send will be clear, concrete, and safe for the client to accept. Initial messages should encourage clients to examine, explore, and take action early in a helping relationship and "should be simple, short-term, and not too demanding" (Purkey & Schmidt, 1996, p. 87). The rationale behind this suggestion is that, as the relationship moves forward and other necessary conditions (such as trust) become stronger, we can create and send more complex and challenging messages.

We are also responsible for acting appropriately. Helpers frequently send messages to tell their clients that something will be done for them. When we make such promises, we must follow through on our pledge. Similarly, when we send messages asking clients to do something, we should ensure that the client understands our message and makes a commitment to carry out the request. When a client accepts our request, we need to follow up to find out how he or she made out. This is an important part of the process that lets clients know we remember our messages and care about how the clients have responded to them. Without assurance that we will clarify and follow through on our commitments and requests, clients may misinterpret our messages and, consequently, become distrustful of our level of care.

Sometimes our messages are not received or clients do not accept them. Knowing how hard to push clients is an important ingredient of intentional caring. As we learned in Chapter 2, clients' perceptions influence their readiness to take risks and make changes in their lives. When we receive a response that says a client is not ready, we respect that position and rethink our original message and clinical position. In a sense, we return to an earlier phase of the helping process: preparing and reading the situation. We reconsider, seek more information from the client and others, and create an alternative message. In this way, we move the helping relationship toward actions that overcome difficulties and obstacles.

Overcoming Obstacles

Despite our best efforts, we are sometimes unsuccessful at reaching out to others. We willingly extend ourselves, create what we believe are caring messages, and send them with the best intentions, only to find that the people we are trying to help reject them. Later in this chapter, we will explore more fully how to care about difficult clients in trying situations. For now, we consider how to handle common obstacles that block our attempts to care. At these times, it is particularly important to examine our intentionality, determine if we are indeed the best helpers to continue a particular relationship, and, if yes, how we need to ensure reception of future helpful messages. By taking these initial steps, we begin to overcome obstacles that prevent our students, clients, and patients from accepting our assistance. In one sense, this is a process of negotiating and compromising to improve our clients' level of comfort.

Negotiation and compromise are part of everyday relationships. For example, when you invite friends to a movie and they decline, the reason may be that the time or date is inconvenient for them. In such a case, you might negotiate a more favorable time by asking, "Would next weekend be better for you?" This type of give-and-take also exists in many other relationships. A supervisor, for example, might ask a worker struggling with an assignment, "If this task is too much for one person, do you have suggestions about how to get it done more efficiently?"

Negotiating and compromising to overcome obstacles require communication skills that incorporate all the ingredients of intentional caring enumerated in this book. They require a positive direction and purpose tempered by an optimistic stance that conveys the message "We can overcome these differences." In addition, because negotiation and compromise should consider the best intentions of everyone involved, they require a trustworthy manner. When we use negotiation and compromise to move our helping relationships forward, we recognize the value of each person in the process.

Occasionally, even the most proficient helpers are unable to resolve differences with particular clients. When this happens, we know how and where to find assistance so that a client's needs can still be met. Professional helpers understand this

Reflection

Experienced helpers understand that messages are sometimes unsuccessful when they are first sent. Confident helpers do not allow temporary obstacles to prevent them from exploring differences and looking for solutions. They use negotiation and compromise to overcome differences and move the relationships forward. When we fail to negotiate differences, the process of helping can end without beneficial results, even though our intentions are good. What qualities do you possess that help or hinder your ability to negotiate and compromise?

ethical responsibility: to seek appropriate supervision or consultation and ensure that every client is referred to appropriate sources when the helping relationship is no longer moving in a positive direction. By behaving so appropriately, we are successful in these cases—not because we resolve the differences that exist or overcome apparent obstacles but because we recognize the limits of our abilities and understand the complexity of all helping relationships. Even in times of frustration and lack of success, we are able to assess accomplishments with clients and measure the progress made in our helping relationships.

Measuring Progress

The value of every helping relationship, every caring act, is measured by what the experience means to both the helper and the client. Sometimes the full value of a helping relationship or a simple caring act might not be measured immediately; the impact may take years to be fully realized. What we hope to see in most of our relationships is progress toward intended goals. For example, a school counselor who is working with a student to improve self-concept is unlikely to see quick results because self-beliefs take time to examine, reflect on, and alter. A person's self-concept is relatively stable (Purkey, 1970, 2000), although counseling and other beneficial experiences can eventually contribute to significant changes in how people see themselves and their world. In the short time they have together, the school counselor and the student hope to begin the process of self-assessment, examine perceptions that need to be rethought, and choose new behaviors that might reinforce more positive self-views. The value of this helping relationship is measured by the progress the counselor and the student make toward these goals.

Intentional helpers are accountable to the people they assist. They are also accountable to themselves as helpers and to the institutions or organizations that employ and use them as professional helpers. At the same time, caring helpers understand that their clients are responsible for what they themselves choose to do, or not to do, in making progress toward chosen goals. This aspect of shared responsibility within the evaluation process is part of the intentional respect already emphasized in this chapter. Because helpers and clients share responsibility for progress in their relationships, they also share the joy when positive results occur or sadness when setbacks happen. Caring relationships include both the hope of success and the risk of failure. When success is realized, progress is usually obvious and easily measured. When setbacks occur, however, we find it more challenging to stop and assess what is happening, evaluate the damage done to progress already made, and decide how to continue proceeding positively.

Successful helpers consistently measure the value and progress of their relationships; it is inherent in their intentionality to do so. They avoid blaming themselves, others, or situations when relationships fail to show the progress expected. Rather, they evaluate objectively with their clients and supervisors and make reasonable decisions about how to move forward. Thus, they continue to create caring messages that demonstrate their desire to help, illustrate the importance of being prepared for various events, convey understanding of how messages are sent and received within helping relationships, and resolve to help clients overcome obstacles that might interfere with their progress. Such actions are particularly essential when caring about clients and patients who present particularly difficult situations or inherently challenge the helping process.

CARING IN DIFFICULT SITUATIONS

Caring messages can assist in a broad array of helping relationships. The process is most useful and appropriate when used with clients who are dealing with normal developmental concerns in their lives or are facing relatively common conflicts and decisions. At times, however, professional helpers assist clients who are struggling with particularly unwieldy situations or have adopted resistant postures to the helping process. The professional literature sometimes refers to such cases as "difficult clients" (Kottler, 1992, 1997; Seligman & Gaaserud, 1994). In such cases, the difficulty generally arises not from the clients themselves but from the challenging social, psychological, or physiological situations they present. These situations might not respond readily to popular approaches in the professional helping literature, particularly when clients are socially and psychologically disturbed. In such instances, relying solely on traditional therapies is not only insufficient but may be neglectful because we delay using more effective means of helping.

Magid and McKelvey (1989) have referred to these difficult clients as "trust bandits," who, because of serious breaks in attachment, have developed "feelings of anger and rage, grief and hopelessness, poor impulse control and a failure to learn the basic social and cognitive skills necessary for a healthy life" (p. 194). Furthermore, they have contended that "of the choices of traditional therapies available . . . all of them fall short when dealing with the true Trust Bandit" (pp. 196–197).

All professional helpers who are working with difficult clients in challenging situations must first make a thorough assessment and determine accurately whether they have the expertise, skill, and competence to be of assistance. If we determine that we can offer these clients appropriate assistance, the process of creating caring messages still applies. Although we might want to create more structure in the process, the fundamental stages of desiring, preparing, sending, receiving, overcoming obstacles, and measuring progress provide the overall framework for the helping relationship.

Guidelines for Creating Caring Messages

Jeffrey Kottler (1997) has listed eight rules of engagement that all helpers might find useful in working with difficult clients. The first rule is *detachment without withdrawal*. Sometimes it is helpful to step back from a relationship particularly when we feel overly involved or when it is becoming too intense. Sometimes difficult cases can feel personally or professionally threatening, and we need to distance ourselves without lessening our care and concern for our clients.

Talking to ourselves is the second guideline. It encourages the use of repeated words or phrases that, when used as mantras, can help relieve stress and maintain our focus on staying relaxed with a client during the session. For example, when an enraged client verbally attacks a therapist, the helper might repeat the unspoken phrase "It is good that I am helping" as a way of diminishing personal feelings of hurt and avoiding an inappropriate response.

Stop complaining is the third guideline and is particularly useful to helpers who work for institutions such as mental health centers, hospitals, and schools. "Sitting around complaining and whining about how awful [clients] are and how they don't care will win you sympathy for a minute or two; after that, you will just continue to feel like a victim" (p. 39). Kottler (1997) has suggested that, rather than complain about negative behaviors or aspects of the case, we should look for positive points to highlight with colleagues, which might engage them in constructive discussions of how to proceed.

The fourth guideline is to *keep our sense of humor*. Humor can help clients broaden or alter their perspectives or reframe their difficulties more positively (Rutherford, 1994). In the same way, our own sense of humor keeps us upbeat and in a positive frame of mind. We will explore the use of humor further in Chapter 5.

Reframe resistance is the fifth guideline, and it is key to helping in difficult situations. Often, students, clients, and patients become saddled with labels that people use to describe their defiant and difficult behaviors. Teachers refer to acting-out students, parents beg help for their delinquent adolescents, and employers search for ways to encourage apathetic workers. Therapists and other professional helpers often find it useful to reframe these descriptions so that both the clients and the person who made the referral can look at the situation from a new perspective. For example, the student who is acting out in class might be "creating a lively class atmosphere." Likewise, the troubled adolescent might be "testing the system," and the workers are "searching for better ways to perform their jobs." As absurd as the reframe may appear on the surface, it might encourage both parties to begin thinking differently about old challenges.

A trait of helper intentionality that we considered in Chapter 2 is the sixth guideline for working with difficult clients: *be flexible*. Kottler (1997) has summed up its importance: "The simplest solution to sorting out any conflict is to figure out what you are doing that is not working—and don't do that anymore. Do something else" (p. 41). Working and being successful with difficult situations requires a high level of creativity in our caring relationships. When we hold onto ineffective strategies and interventions that challenging clients continue to reject, we maintain an inflexible posture that magnifies the conflict and difficulty within our helping relationships.

Helping squared (that is, adding more helpers) is the seventh guideline for engagement. Kottler (1997) noted that even the most helpful professionals can get stuck with their clients. During these impasses, it might be appropriate to bring in other resources, such as a colleague of the helper or friend of the client, who can provide an objective assessment of the relationship and offer the helper and client suggestions on how to move the process forward.

Reflection

Consider Kottler's (1997) guidelines in the context of your work with difficult clients. Which of them will be most challenging for you to follow?

The eighth and final guideline is to *let go*. It is a myth to believe that every helper is capable of helping every client. Sometimes clients will not work with us. When this becomes clear, we need to recognize the situation and admit that it is best to discontinue the relationship. Ethically, we want to offer these clients the opportunity to seek assistance from other sources, and we can help them with such referrals. However, to continue an ineffective relationship is unwise for them and us.

Strategies and Interventions

Although much has been written about working with difficult clients, keeping a flexible stance that allows you to choose from an array of strategies might be the best approach. In this section, we explore strategies and interventions from several sources. Some are practical ideas, while others are more theoretical. All are included here because they relate to qualities and factors associated with creating caring messages. Combined with the guidelines for engagement just discussed, these strategies and interventions can help you create successful helping relationships in challenging situations.

- *Break bread*. Sharing food as a way of becoming acquainted is a tradition that crosses many cultures. Offering snacks and beverages to clients is a sign of hospitality that helps set a comfortable tone for any helping relationship.
- *Lower your rank*. Forming a collaborative relationship to work toward common goals is more facilitative than taking an authoritative posture. During helping relationships, it is sometimes appropriate to demonstrate one's expertise and position; but with difficult clients, it might be best not to begin by asserting authority.
- *Begin with the person*. Become familiar with the client as a person, not simply as a difficult case. Learn about interests, tastes, and other personal traits and share yours when appropriate. By starting the process on a personal level, we create an atmosphere in which clients are willing to share concerns and problems.
- *Explain the helping process*. People need to know that by being involved in a helping relationship, they will reap some benefit. Sometimes clients feel helpless. Therefore, learning about the helping process and the control they have may give them a feeling of empowerment.
- *Look toward the future*. Although past events may be contributing factors and present behaviors might drive other people crazy, we can best help clients by focusing on what they want to see happen in their lives.

- *Respect the client's expertise*. No one knows clients better than they know themselves. Let them hear that their perceptions, beliefs, and self-knowledge are valuable pieces of information that are essential to the success of the helping.

- *Accept that everyone is motivated*. It is a fallacy to think that some students and clients are unmotivated. Everyone is motivated in some way and in some direction. Although difficult clients might illustrate their motivation in contrary ways, they are nevertheless motivated. A key to being successful with these clients is to help them determine if they are motivated in a direction that is beneficial to them.

- *Take one step at a time*. Difficult clients did not become that way overnight; their life situation has developed over a period of time. Consequently, we cannot expect major changes to occur quickly. Some clients, however, are impatient, so we need to focus on small steps that they can succeed in taking and celebrate those accomplishments as we work toward larger goals.

- *Monitor for cultural differences*. As with all our clients, we must accept and be respectful of cultural diversity and understand how clients' cultural traditions and heritage might interact with their present difficulties. Learning about their backgrounds and providing a safe environment in which to examine the importance of culture in one's identity are essential to every helping relationship.

- *Challenge self-deprecating behavior*. Positive-thinking people are rarely difficult clients. Difficult clients, on the other hand, often have negative thoughts about themselves and other people. Gentle confrontation is appropriate in these instances and is a way to encourage more optimistic thinking. As Seligman (1992) has explained, "changing the destructive things you say to yourself when you experience setbacks that life deals all of us is the central skill of optimism" (p. 7). By pointing out contradictions to negative self-talk and highlighting the strengths a particular client has shown during the early stages of the helping relationship, we take a step in this direction.

- *Keep your comments short and understandable*. Lengthy explanations and comments will be lost on most clients. Those with short attention spans or people who are easily distracted will be lost even sooner. Stay in tune by giving short directions and suggestions using language and vocabulary that are developmentally appropriate.

- *Celebrate progress*. Ask clients if they see progress in reaching their goals. Take time in the helping process to celebrate steps that have been taken toward these goals.

- *Be available*. Difficult situations sometimes require helpers to be available at unorthodox times. Set reasonable expectations and establish appropriate procedures for clients to get in touch with you.

- *Build a network of support*. As the helping relationship progresses, invite students, clients, and patients to suggest people who could be included in the process. No one can stand alone; and after the helping relationship has ended, clients will need a circle of supportive family, friends, and colleagues to lean on during difficult times in the future.

- *Lend a resource.* Loaning a favorite book or some other resource to a client can be a show of faith that helps establish trusting relationships. It is also a way of sharing something you value that might be helpful to the client in dealing with a difficult situation.
- *Say no gently and slowly.* Sometimes our clients have requests that we cannot fulfill or we do not agree with. Difficult clients have faced rejection throughout their lives and will occasionally test the helping relationship with seemingly outrageous demands simply to watch our reactions. On these occasions, it is helpful to listen fully to the request before making our decision. At the same time, we want to respond firmly but gently when explaining our position.
- *Increase your knowledge.* Difficult clients and challenging situations bring a range of problems and concerns. Learn what the research has said about these situations and what current practices are most efficacious in establishing successful helping relationships.

These strategies and interventions are starters to assist you in working with difficult clients. When using any approach, however, we must attain a high level of empathic understanding (see Figure 4.2). Through greater understanding of our clients and ourselves and by applying appropriate strategies, we can create and send caring messages that will help us work with all clients.

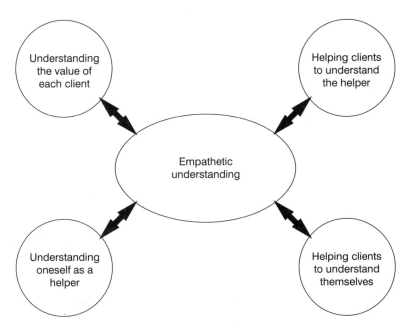

FIGURE 4.2 *Developing understanding with difficult clients*

5

Doing for Oneself What You Expect of Others

*To cope successfully with the reality of everyday living,
we must have a firm grip on our own identity.*

Don Hamachek
Encounters with the Self, 1992, p. 316

In this book, we have illustrated the importance of establishing and maintaining an intentionally caring stance in all helping relationships by examining what it means for us to care, exploring essential elements and traits related to our capacity to care, emphasizing the importance of balancing our care with sufficient knowledge and appropriate skill, and discovering a process with which to monitor and measure the effects of our intentional helping relationships. Throughout this journey we have focused on how we as helpers can best demonstrate our care with and for other people.

In all our helping relationships, we convey an *expectation* to students, clients, and patients. For example, therapists hope their clients will focus on concerns, achieve greater self-awareness, and use this knowledge to make appropriate life changes. Likewise, medical practitioners expect that their patients will follow prescribed treatments that move them toward healthier lifestyles. We and our clients work together, properly caring for, respecting, and accepting each other; and we expect that our clients will make appropriate decisions toward action that move them forward in their life goals.

All the ingredients of caring and helping that we have explored in this book play an important role in enabling us to care for and about other people. An underlying assumption we make in our relationships is that we as helpers are capable of doing for ourselves what we expect of others. That is, if a school counselor helps a student work through feelings of inadequacy regarding class work and school performance, this counselor must be self-assured about her or his own scholarly abilities and pursuits. Likewise, a nutritionist who advises a patient about healthful eating habits probably has his or her own diet under control. In short, caring for others implies a willingness and ability on our part to care for ourselves. It means doing for ourselves what we expect our clients to do in making life more productive and self-fulfilling.

In this chapter, we consider how the elements of caring relate to our development and our healthy life choices. In particular, we examine how self-awareness relates to our ability to care for ourselves and establish everyday helpful relationships with others. Previously, we learned about the importance of self-knowledge in establishing truly caring relationships. Now we will consider how our own self-awareness contributes to our success in daily living as well as in our professional or volunteer roles.

The positive tone of this chapter takes its lead from the work of Abraham Maslow, who focused on human attributes that contribute to the self-actualization of healthy functioning people (Hamachek, 1992). Some schools of psychology have tended to study the human condition from a deficit model, looking at the weaknesses and faults that cause people problems. In contrast, Maslow (1970) investigated factors and traits that seem to enable people to be successful and do great things. In his studies of world leaders, noted scientists, and other historic figures, Maslow identified several basic qualities that distinguish self-actualized people. Although his list is a compendium of qualities and is not intended to imply that successful people possess every trait, it does suggest that the historical figures under study "did exhibit a greater number of these characteristics and in more different ways than might be expected in a less self-actualized person" (Hamachek, 1992, p. 96).

Following is a summary of Maslow's characteristics of self-actualized people, describing behaviors typically illustrating characteristics that contribute to and enrich the process of self-actualization:

- Being realistically oriented and accepting themselves, others, and the world around them as they are
- Maintaining a spontaneous disposition yet attending to the task at hand and closely identifying with a particular mission or duty in life
- Occasionally seeking privacy, usually to concentrate on important matters or subjects of intense interest
- Remaining independent and self-reliant even when confronted by rejection and unpopularity
- Appreciating the basic qualities of life and a capacity to enjoy the simple pleasures
- Experiencing frequent visionary or spiritual episodes, although not necessarily of a religious nature, and having a strong sense of ethical responsibility

Reflection

Beyond your knowledge and skill, what qualifies you to be a caring helper? By answering this question, you will begin to examine the genuineness you bring to all helping relationships.

- Identifying with the human race as a whole and being concerned about the entire world
- Having genuine loving relationships with a few people, which tend to be heartfelt and deeply emotional
- Judging people democratically on the basis of who they are and what they do rather than on racial, religious, or similar characteristics
- Conveying a respectful sense of humor
- Being blessed with a gift for creativity and resisting conventional wisdom

The essential traits of caring helpers are woven into this list of self-actualizing characteristics. For each of us, therefore, an examination of these qualities may help us assess our own level of self-awareness and measure our willingness to do for ourselves what we expect of others.

REFLECTING ACCURATELY

By considering Maslow's characteristics of self-actualized people, we can reflect on our own strengths as caring helpers. Taking time to think about who we are, consistently assessing what encourages us to reach out and care for other people, and reflecting on the knowledge and skill we use to establish our helping relationships are worthwhile activities that ensure honorable intentions and ethical practice. They also ensure that we meet our own expectation for a high standard of helping.

In this section, we consider five categories that can help us reflect on our motivations and behaviors in caring relationships. The categories combine many of Maslow's (1970) characteristics of self-actualization. Keep in mind that these categories convey my own perception of Maslow's characteristics, so you might find some differences in the way you categorize these ideas yourself. But since Maslow's research showed that successful people exhibit these qualities in different ways, we might similarly expect successful helpers to have varying perspectives on what each characteristic means for them personally and professionally.

Groundedness

Successful helpers are grounded in a realistic view of themselves, others, and the world in a way that gives them a sound basis on which to care for people. Although this broad view is generally stable, helpers are willing to examine, reflect on, and alter it as they test new information and prove it to be credible. In this way, they maintain a sound footing in a belief system that is based on common knowledge and accepted practices.

In some respects, our firm stance reflects the "knowing" that, according to Mayeroff (1971), is an essential aspect of caring. He suggests, "To care for someone I must *know* many things" (p. 13). Thus, to be an effective helper, we must know our clients, ourselves, and appropriate ways of helping. Furthermore, we use this knowledge in a genuine manner, even when being this "real" may make us uncomfortable

(Rogers, 1961). Being grounded means that we keep the best interests of students, clients, and patients in the forefront of our efforts to help them.

To remain firmly established in a reality that is both knowing and caring, we are also open to changing events and new information. Scientific discoveries, innovative technology, and a host of possibilities exist now and in the future, and each will have the potential to influence our helping relationships, whether we work in communicative therapies or more scientific fields. If we are uncompromising in our convictions and strategies, we may miss opportunities in the changing reality. To avoid such omission, we allow ourselves to dream and envision new ways of functioning that take us to higher levels of caring. Caring people use their imagination in the same way that artists are moved by visions of what they can create. Similarly, gifted athletes often see the results of their moves before they actually hit the ball, take the shot, or start the race. Sometimes these creative visions have underlying spiritual or religious meaning. If so, we should be cautiously private about these motivations so as not to impose our beliefs on other people.

Our willingness to envision change and alter past ways of helping is a sign of our spontaneity. Because we are grounded in a healthy belief system, the spontaneous behaviors we choose are just that—spontaneous. Without a firm footing and genuine realness about what to do in our helping relationships, we would not be able to function so spontaneously. Instead, we would flounder behaviorally, causing chaos among students, clients, and patients. By the same token, without a firm understanding of what our role is, we might not maintain a clear focus on our mission or attend to routine tasks within our helping relationships.

Being grounded in a philosophy of helping and being real with oneself and others also relate to ethical practice. Nel Noddings (1984) defined the *ethical self* as "an active relation between my actual self and vision of my ideal self" (p. 49). By reflecting on our present helping behaviors and consistently challenging ourselves to act in the most ethical manner, we also guard against becoming too rigid and locked into a single mode of helping for every client. As we have already learned, this flexibility indicates a high degree of intentionality as effective helpers (Ivey & Ivey, 1998).

We expect our clients to view their own concerns and challenges realistically. To facilitate such a helping relationship, we, too, must keep an even keel in our lives. Having a dependable point of view, basing our actions on a realistic orientation, and maintaining a degree of flexibility and spontaneity in our relationships are ways to exemplify a firm yet healthy foundation for caring.

Reflection

How has technological innovation changed your life? Think of how you have adapted to the new technology and contemplate your willingness to adapt to other life changes.

Autonomy

In caring relationships, we strive to help clients become more independent and self-reliant. Even though students, clients, and patients rely on us for encouragement and support throughout the helping process, their ultimate goal is to achieve freedom from dependency on others. In all human endeavors and encounters, having support from and involvement with other people is psychologically and socially healthy; but everyone needs to establish her or his own identity. For clients, such an identity includes complete confidence in who they are, where they are going, and what they want to become. As we have learned, caring relationships facilitate a search for freedom and autonomy.

Because competent counselors, nurses, social workers, therapists, and other helpers attain a level of self-assuredness and strength in their convictions, they have the courage to help clients make educational, career, and life-altering decisions. We accomplish this goal by first seeking approval and affirmation from our inner selves and then trusting that our decisions will win the approval of people who are important to us.

Approval from others, however, is not paramount to our decisions. To be truly free and independent, we understand that sometimes our choices and our support of others might lead other people to reject or disapprove of us. For example, a mental health counselor who opposes a new policy because it places unnecessary hardship on clients might anger co-workers who want the regulation for their own convenience. As caring helpers, we consistently and dependably take stands that not only demonstrate our self-reliance but also contribute to the equitable treatment of everyone in the community.

At the same time, we balance our striving for independence with a genuine regard for the opinions and feelings of other people. If we make all our decisions in isolation, we may lose sight of what is socially important and acceptable. In such a case, we may move from a posture of self-reliance to one of tyranny. According to Maslow (1970), a valuable characteristic of successful leaders is their ability to deal with people equitably and democratically. Such a perspective balances our own need for autonomy and the interests of the people we are trying to help. Adjusting our decisiveness and independence to ensure the welfare of everyone involved is a sign of psychological health and well-being, which are essential to all caring relationships.

In a sense, appropriate striving for autonomy permits us to get closer to students, clients, and patients. Although this reasoning might sound paradoxical, the

Reflection

What does autonomy mean for us as helpers? If we work to help other people free themselves from emotional ties that unwisely bind them to dependent relationships, are we capable of doing the same for ourselves?

Reflection

Assess your own autonomy. Do rituals or traditions bind you to behaviors that restrict your freedom of choice? What can you do to change these patterns?

more self-confident and assured we are as helpers, the more capable we become of moving into clients' private worlds, letting ourselves feel their emotions, and truly empathizing with them. In contrast, the less self-reliant we are, the more dependent we might become on others. Such dependency and need for approval can make it difficult for us to demonstrate genuine empathy and care.

As caring helpers, we understand the need to remain independent—but not at the expense of our clients and certainly not at all cost. Our autonomy and freedom are essential elements in creating caring relationships because they enable us to be self-assured in determining a direction and purpose for helping while allowing clients to affirm themselves and achieve greater self-reliance.

Humor

Although being a helper can exact both a physical and psychological toll, the axiom "laughter is the best medicine" does apply in some helping relationships. By maintaining a sense of humor, we keep ourselves in a positive frame of mind and thus maintain the optimism necessary for an encouraging stance. At the same time, humor and laughter have been shown to produce beneficial physiological effects, allowing us to release tension and find joy in life (Lefcourt & Martin, 1986; Wooten, 1992). Norman Cousins (1979), one of the first popular authors to draw attention to the power of humor and laughter, spent several years at the UCLA Medical School researching the effects of humor. Since then, many other researchers have reported relationships between laughter and renewed energy, stimulation of the immune system, cathartic release, and many other beneficial effects (Berk, 1989; Goodheart, 1994; Wooten, 1994).

Nevertheless, we must maintain respect while sharing the funny side of life. Always, we avoid using humor to degrade, belittle, or otherwise show disrespect for other people. Sarcasm, cynicism, obscenity, and similar approaches are not helpful and do not convey the elements of caring that we have considered in this book. The laughter we encourage is never at the expense of others.

Mosak and Maniacci (1993) have proposed five specific uses of humor in professional helping relationships. First, humor can help clients and patients feel comfortable with the helping process. Second, by observing how clients use humor (i.e., "Does the client laugh with other people or laugh at them?"), we can assess aspects of their personality and how they express emotions. Third, humor can be a bridge to confrontation, pointing out areas of concern that may need the client's attention.

Fourth, humorous exaggeration of life's problems may help clients put their own concerns in perspective. For example, a nurse comforting a patient in a leg splint might joke about being in a full-body cast instead. Finally, when clients are able to achieve a respectful sense of humor and attain a healthy perspective on their concerns, we as helpers are moving the helping relationship toward a productive closure.

How we use humor to share aspects of ourselves indicates our own psychological health. When we are comfortable about laughing over our foibles and mishaps, we demonstrate a level of self-assuredness and openness. Sometimes we expect clients to see humor in the circumstances surrounding their concerns. Therefore, it seems reasonable to achieve this level ourselves. Poking fun at ourselves in a respectful manner lets us take a break from the serious work we do as helpers. Without such respites, we might become so entrenched in the stressful, taxing, and sometimes morbid circumstances of our work that we lose effectiveness as caring helpers.

Being silly, sharing funny stories, and using hyperbole are ways to open part of ourselves to others. Our humor illustrates authenticity, which for counselors and other helpers is essential to creating intentionally caring relationships (Frakes, 1999). It also indicates the degree to which we are enjoying life.

Enjoyment

In all our helping relationships, we have a common goal of bringing some level of enjoyment to people's lives despite their individual circumstances. In nursing, for example, such enjoyment might result from helping a patient find pleasure in life regardless of a terminal illness. Helping students, clients, and patients identify for themselves aspects of their lives that give them satisfaction and enjoyment is essential in any relationship.

By the same token, we demonstrate caring for ourselves by seeking enjoyment away from the helping relationships that are an important part of our daily work. In a sense, we manage our caring so that we give ourselves relief from what may seem at times to be overwhelming challenges. Being in the company of people we love, sharing fun experiences with friends and colleagues, and taking time for ourselves to enjoy simple pleasures of life are valuable activities that rejuvenate our soul and enable us to maintain optimism during difficult situations.

When our professional lives or volunteer services consume so much time and energy that we neglect relationships important to our own well-being, our priorities are out of alignment. When this happens, a measure of our own health is the capability we have to step back, assess the situation, and take appropriate action on behalf of ourselves. This is what we ask of our clients and therefore what we are willing to do for ourselves. Renewing interest in a hobby or a musical instrument we once enjoyed, taking time to meditate and reenergize, and bringing together friends who have not socialized recently are a few examples of the countless ways we focus attention on enjoying life. Like humor, enjoyment contributes to our total health; and like the other characteristics and traits that enable us to care, both must become integral parts of our own lives. As C. Gilbert Wrenn (1973) instructed, "to care for yourself means acknowledging all of you and acknowledging that one part of self is dependent on the whole" (p. 284).

Self-Acceptance

We care for ourselves by achieving a level of self-acceptance that reinforces our ability to be effective helpers, just as we expect clients to minimize their faults and maximize their usefulness. By recognizing our value as helpers, we clarify and recognize our role as well as the skills and abilities that define what we do. At the same time, we identify the limitations of our professional and volunteer functions, thus ensuring that we use only helpful behaviors and interventions within the scope of our preparation and ethical practice. These limitations are not permanent because we are always seeking to renew our knowledge and update our skills. As such, continued learning is an important aspect of the acceptance we demonstrate toward ourselves as caring helpers.

Another element of our acceptance is the degree to which we show favor to all people and groups regardless of who they are, where they come from, or what they do. Maslow (1970) alluded to this important trait in his study of successful people and world leaders. He found that leaders and other noted people not only accepted who they were but also demonstrated broad respect for other persons and the environment. How we convey such acceptance can take countless forms. For this reason, we as helpers must be keenly aware of our overt behaviors, language, unintentional gestures, and other idiosyncratic actions that might convey nonacceptance. For example, a teacher I once knew habitually moved her lips as I was talking, echoing and sometimes anticipating what I was saying. Although I cannot assess how this behavior affected her ability to listen, I recall that the mannerism distracted me. I also wondered how persons from other cultures might interpret this behavior. As noted, caring helpers work with a wide range of people from various backgrounds and cultures. To be successful with all clients, we must be sure that our acceptance is evident to everyone with whom we work and live.

The key is to be comfortable with ourselves—speaking and behaving confidently, treating ourselves respectfully, and accepting who we are not as a permanent condition but as a point of departure for those traits and characteristics we want to alter. This level of self-acceptance is essential if we are going to be able to care intentionally for ourselves.

Reflection

Self-criticism and self-doubt are great inhibitors that limit our willingness to reach out to others. Finding ways to maintain positive and accurate views of your abilities as a helper is essential. How would you begin?

CARING FOR ONESELF

A universal goal in all helping relationships is encouraging our clients to take care of themselves. Therefore, it must also be an expectation for ourselves. As noted, helpful persons sometimes spend so much time and energy caring for others that they risk neglecting themselves. This pattern is not optimal for establishing consistently and dependably caring relationships because it sends conflicting messages about our genuine belief in the caring process. For example, a nurse who fails to follow sound advice about adhering to prescription instructions sends the message that he is not a credible role model for patients. Similarly, a mental health counselor who refuses help in handling a personal crisis cannot expect clients to enter counseling relationships willingly.

We have considered the important contribution that knowledge and skill make to caring relationships and how maintaining knowledge and skill enables us to function at a high professional level. Likewise, caring about ourselves on a personal level helps us maintain an emotional, physical, and spiritual health that is vital to caring relationships. Caregivers who are emotionally capable, physically fit, and spiritually at peace are more able to have the psychological strength, physical stamina, and inner calmness to care about and for other people.

Emotional and Psychological Health

Caring helpers attend to how they think of themselves and understand that healthy internal dialogue—what we sometimes call "self-talk"—emanates from healthy thoughts. Findings in cognitive behavioral research suggest that, when we are healthy, we tell ourselves to behave in responsible, respectful, and caring ways (Purkey, 2000). We focus on constructive thoughts and minimize negative thinking. We also tend to associate with people who maintain positive attitudes and optimistic views of life. These associations encourage us and affirm the attributes and qualities we see in ourselves that enable us to be successful caregivers. In this way, we become the successful helpers we *think* we can be.

As helpers, we often encourage students, clients, and patients to accept support from other people—friends, family, colleagues, and professionals. In taking charge of our emotional selves, we also seek support from other people. This support comes in a variety of forms, such as friendships, family relations, mentoring, and collegial activities.

Friends are frequently a reflection of ourselves; and when we think of ourselves in healthy ways, we affirm the value and worth of our friendships. Usually, we can accept personal evaluations from friends whom we trust. For example, when we neglect some aspect of life, such as eating properly, a trusted friend might encourage us to examine this problem and take corrective action. If we regard our friend's opinion, we are more likely to take heed than we might be when receiving advice from a stranger or someone whose opinions we do not value. Without close friendships to guide us through stressful and difficult times, we might rely on destructive, negative self-talk that prevents us from caring about others and ourselves. "Pessimistic prophesies are self-fulfilling" (Seligman, 1992, p. 7).

Reflection

When you needed help in your life, where did you turn? Was the help you sought useful to you? If so, why?

We seek support from others through cherished family relations, intimate friendships, and respected collegial guidance. At the same time, because we understand the value of professional helping and realize that an array of factors contributes to or detracts from our emotional well-being, we willingly seek support from counselors, therapists, medical professionals, and other helpers when needed. Just as we expect our clients to relate comfortably to us in the helping relationship, we experience that same comfort when we seek counseling, medical attention, or other services.

Physical Health

Because emotional well-being is often linked to physical health, we care for ourselves physically to maintain our stamina for coping with stressful events. The same strategies we recommend to clients help us maintain our strength, reduce tension and fatigue, and remain focused during difficult times (Hilyer, Jenkins, Deaton, Dillon, Meadows, & Wilson, 1980; Hinkle, 1988). When we are constantly fatigued, undernourished, or under stress, it is difficult to care about others dependably and responsibly because our thought processes are not functioning at optimal levels. Low physical functioning detracts from effective helping (Aspy, Roebuck, & Aspy, 1983). Thus, regular exercise, sound eating habits, routine medical checkups, and proper rest are requirements for keeping ourselves fit. In addition, coping skills such as relaxation techniques, breathing exercises, and meditation are fundamental strategies for redirecting our thoughts toward more positive, constructive goals.

As helpers, we know that controlling thoughts is not an easy task. If it were, people might not need the services of counselors, therapists, and similar professionals. Limitless factors challenge us to think well of other people and ourselves, particularly when people are difficult or situations are demanding. Uncaring people, frustrating events, untimely accidents, and other circumstances can get in our way. Developing routines to care consistently for our physical selves can give us stamina to withstand daily challenges and unpredictable situations. Reading about ways to maintain a healthy lifestyle, attending seminars, and listening to instructional tapes can help us establish patterns for positive self-talk. Similarly, self-help materials and workshops encourage us to monitor our diet, avoid overindulgence, exercise appropriately, participate in athletic activities, and follow medical instructions. The expectations we have of our clients not to be controlled by addictions to exercise, food, alcohol, or other substances are also expectations we have for ourselves. In this way we take charge of our lives and maintain self-control.

Spiritual Well-Being

For many of us, caring is an aspect of our spiritual being. But whether or not caring is part of strong religious beliefs, it is guided by an assumption that something beyond our physical being connects all people in a meaningful way (Gladding, 1996). For some, spirituality is the cultivation of a life in which they exhibit genuine caring for people in mutually beneficial ways. It may or may not include beliefs in a divine power; but if it does, this spirituality encourages us to exhibit unconditional regard for all people regardless of religious differences. When we cultivate a spiritual life, we are positioned to demonstrate consistent concern and care for others as well as ourselves.

Caring about and for others is incorporated into our helping relationships with students, clients, and patients. Helping relationships that neglect to encourage clients to use their new skills and behaviors to strengthen and enrich relations with other people seem unfinished at best. For example, a mental health counselor who successfully leads a group of adolescents in learning problem-solving behaviors does a great service to the community when the members leave the group encouraged to return to their schools and neighborhoods to help fellow students, teachers, parents, friends, and others. They use these skills to resolve conflicts peaceably, tackle environmental issues, and address other significant problems in their lives. Likewise, we maintain this expectation for ourselves. The helping skills we use in our professional and volunteer relationships are also valuable in tending to important relationships in our own lives. We nurture a few intimate relationships, establish social relationships to enjoy life, and form professional alliances that strengthen the knowledge and skills essential to our helping relationships.

TENDING TO RELATIONSHIPS

Philosopher Eric Fromm (1970) observed that the "affirmation of one's life, happiness, growth, freedom is rooted in one's capacity to love, i.e., in care, respect, responsibility, and knowledge" (p. 50). Although everyone benefits from loving relationships, we as caregivers become more articulate in our helping relationships to the degree that we manage and cultivate personal and intimate relations ourselves. At the same time, our capacity to be with others in caring and loving ways correlates with our ability to relate with an inner self.

In addition to establishing intimate relationships, we care for ourselves personally by socializing with friends, family, and colleagues in ways that allow us to be in the company of others. As human beings, we need these associations. By sharing experiences, interacting with people, and celebrating life's events, we demonstrate ways of taking care of ourselves personally. Such interactions can also help us broaden our perception about important issues if we consciously expand our social circle to include people who are rich in diversity. As caring helpers, we make every attempt to be open to new ideas and accept other people's views. In contrast, if we severely limit our social interactions, we may restrict our vision of life's possibilities. This could have negative consequences for our tolerance of human differences, an

Reflection

Assess the diversity of people in your life. When you look at your closest professional and personal relationships, what diversity do you see?

outcome that would be detrimental to our effectiveness with clients from divergent backgrounds and cultures.

Professional relationships are also important to our development as caring helpers. As in personal relationships, professional caring for oneself takes the form of either individual activities or interactions with other professionals from and with whom we can learn.

Invitational counseling (Purkey & Schmidt, 1996) offers a structure with which to assess and monitor four quadrants of tending to personal and professional relations, which I have adapted here: (1) caring about oneself personally, (2) caring about others personally, (3) caring about oneself professionally, and (4) caring about others professionally.

Caring About Oneself Personally

In this chapter, we have already considered many aspects of caring about ourselves personally. For example, taking care of ourselves physically, emotionally, and spiritually keeps us healthy and in tune with our inner selves. Throughout this book, we have emphasized a fundamental premise that, to care about others consistently and reliably, we must care about ourselves. We expect students, clients, and patients to take proper care of themselves by balancing commitment to work and family and monitoring their personal well-being. In the same way, we keep ourselves in top form by taking time for ourselves, accepting responsibility for our actions, assessing our stress level, seeking support from others when appropriate, and treating ourselves with the same level of care that we treat our clients.

To assess our state of personal well-being, we might ask ourselves questions in much the same way that we gather information from clients. For example, when considering our physical state, we might wonder about muscle spasms or pains, dizzy spells, rashes, headaches, high blood pressure, back problems, chest pains, or other discomfort that needs our attention. Similarly, we might assess signs of fatigue, forgetfulness, impatience, or lack of concentration that may emanate from physical causes. In all these instances, we need to seek appropriate assistance to ensure proper care for ourselves.

Another realm of personal caring involves the time we give to ourselves. It is helpful to spend time alone in meditation, self-reflection, and solitude. As active caregivers, we are often in demand, providing services and tending to the needs of others. By taking some time for ourselves, we are able to examine our accomplishments, assess future goals, design plans to reach these goals, and gather thoughts about our personal well-being and happiness. For example, time alone spent reading for enjoyment, taking quiet walks, meditating, or listening to music keeps us in touch with our inner selves, helps us evaluate our personal and professional goals, and assess our satisfaction with life.

Caring About Others Personally

We are all social beings and want to belong (Sweeney, 1998). Many of the problems people experience begin with their fear of not being accepted or valued by the people with whom they want to associate. People who fail to achieve some sense of belonging in their lives remain unfulfilled and become discontented, fearful, and dissatisfied.

In most helping situations, we encourage clients to establish relationships with other people because the personal support they receive from such encounters can be beneficial. By the same token, we as helpers should share the company of others. Professional and volunteer helpers have a special need to develop and cultivate social relationships because through this process we strengthen our ability to establish trusting relationships. The wider we spread these interactions, the greater our tolerance for different cultures, uncustomary behaviors, and unfamiliar world views. When we limit our social interactions to a few family members and friends who think and behave in familiar ways, we limit possibilities and opportunities that could enrich our lives and contribute to a caring and consistent posture for effective helping.

By extending ourselves personally within a broad circle of acquaintances and friends, we establish a framework for a healthy social life, paralleling our expectations for students, clients, and patients. The broader our social frame of reference, the stronger and more reliable our most trusting personal relationships become.

One way to expand our personal caring is to seek out people who seem isolated or alone. This takes thoughtful consideration because, as noted, creating positive messages means accurately reading situations. The first hurdle to overcome when extending ourselves to others is eliminating anxieties related to apparent differences. Once we overcome this obstacle, we can begin to look for advantages of relating with people in new and different situations.

Caring About Oneself Professionally

A repeated theme of this book is that dependable caring requires humane and compassionate qualities balanced with competent skill and knowledge. Most helping professionals and volunteers recognize the need to keep their knowledge current and their skills fine-tuned. To maintain a credible position with clients, we stay up to date with our particular fields of helping.

As counselors, nurses, social workers, and other helpers, our learning is continuous. We read professional journals, attend conferences and workshops, present and publish research findings for colleagues, and pursue further study. Through these various activities we keep ourselves abreast of trends and developments in our field and avoid becoming outdated in our knowledge and skill.

Professional involvement is another important aspect of caring about ourselves professionally. In each helping specialty, professional associations and organizations inform members, provide educational opportunities, establish standards of practice, and create other opportunities for professional development. Active involvement and participation in our professional associations are ways to remain current and credible as caring helpers. Through our participation with associations and organizations we also form friendships and alliances that support and strengthen our professional growth.

One area of professional caring that has become increasingly important in some fields of helping is clinical supervision (Ronnestad & Skovholt, 1993; Williams, 1987). Helpers in various fields sometimes work alone without either support or colleagues to use as sounding boards for advice. Counselors, social workers, therapists, and other professionals who care about their practice seek out opportunities to increase their clinical supervision. For example, consider an elementary school counselor working without colleagues or adequate supervision. Because she cares about herself professionally, this counselor seeks supervision by creating a peer supervision model in her system or establishing a collaborative relationship with a local mental health counselor and counselor educator at a nearby university. The purpose of these relationships is to establish a supportive environment in which one's clinical skills and approaches to helping can be assessed and constructive feedback offered.

Caring About Others Professionally

Caring about others professionally and caring about oneself personally and professionally enable us to care about others professionally. Each of the four areas under discussion interacts with the others. Over many years, William Purkey and I have discussed and asked questions about this interactive process. For example, we have wondered, Does one have to be personally caring before being professionally caring? In this discussion, we have discovered our different perspectives about this question. As a helping professional or volunteer, you will probably arrive at your own answer, and it will influence how you approach helping relationships.

We can all recount experiences with professionals who seemed to lack personal awareness or attributes that helped them relate to other people. For example, consider a high school mathematics teacher who knows the subject matter and can convey complicated concepts to students but lacks the ability (or desire) to care about others personally. The teacher distances herself from students to the point where it

Reflection

Can you be a successful helper in professional relationships without tending to your personal needs and career development?

sometimes appears she does not care about them. Yet they learn the mathematical concepts and skills required to move forward. Might the teacher be more effective and successful with all her students if she demonstrates an appropriate level of personal caring? Any answer is pure conjecture, but the question is worth pondering as each of us examines our own beliefs about these four areas of caring.

Professionally caring for others also returns us to the fundamental importance of our knowledge and skill as helpers. This point highlights the interaction between caring professionally for ourselves to assure our competency in caring about others. In addition, professional caring includes proactive behaviors that are demonstrated by how we cooperate and collaborate with others and how we contribute to the welfare of those who seek our help (Purkey & Schmidt, 1996).

We cooperate by forming alliances with other helpers to facilitate processes and break down traditional barriers for the benefit of students, clients, and patients. Similarly, we collaborate by working together to combine our knowledge and skill, thus increasing our likelihood of success. Lastly, we care professionally by contributing to our institution and community beyond the normal expectations that people might have for our role in helping relationships. In Chapter 6, we consider this notion of caring beyond the typical helping relationship.

6

Beyond the Helping Relationship

A change in a person inevitably affects society as well.

Arthur W. Combs and David M. Gonzalez
Helping Relationships, 1994, p. 217

This book has focused on aspects of caring that influence not only our helping relationships with students, clients, and patients but also ourselves. Reaching out to people, advocating for changes in our institutions, and expressing unconditional love are not unique to intentional helping. Many scholars and authors, including Carl Rogers, C. Gilbert Wrenn, Leo Buscaglia, Eric Fromm, Rollo May, and William Purkey, have believed that these attributes are essential for all capable helpers and fully functioning people. In this chapter, we examine how to use these aspects of caring to extend beyond individual relationships to a larger audience. Here we consider how to use our knowledge and skills to encourage clients to care for others, to challenge institutions to relate and operate with greater care, and to nurture loving relationships that expand beyond present alliances.

CULTIVATING CARE FOR OTHERS

In most helping relationships, our clients establish goals that apply to their daily interactions, where they move forward with their accomplishments. For example, a client's newly acquired coping skills can be used to help other people if clients extend themselves through volunteer services, support groups, self-help programs, and other venues. Cancer survivors, for instance, can care for other patients by informing them about medical procedures, leading support groups for the terminally or chronically ill, and sharing strategies they have found helpful for coping with chemotherapy or other treatments. Learning to extend helping relationships is especially useful for clients who face everyday challenges, decisions, and difficulties. Nevertheless, we always remember to avoid even the appearance of client obligation. Such an approach is unethical. Exposing clients to opportunities for helping others is one thing, but coercing or obliging them to reach out is a gross misuse of our helping role.

In my field of educational counseling, we extend the helping relationship when we use students, teachers, and parents to disseminate information and provide support to the larger school community. Peer helper programs, teacher advisor programs, and parent education groups are examples of structures that counselors use in schools to encourage extended helping relationships. Alfie Kohn (1991) addressed the need for schools to cultivate caring by using group experiences, and group counseling authorities validate this view by asserting that one advantage of group process in schools is that it creates a setting in which group members help one another (Gladding, 1999).

This philosophy need not be restricted to educational settings. Mental health counselors, social workers, nurses, and other helpers from a wide range of clinical settings can include their clients in volunteer and professional caregiving. Significant to all these relationships is the fact that we seek broad support for our clients while we facilitate individual helping processes with them. We engender the same reliance on support systems when they move toward closure with us. How we close these helping relationships and cultivate a desire within our clients to reach out and care about others who are facing similar concerns is a worthy consideration in a democratic society. It may seem like an awesome responsibility for helpers who work with difficult clients in trying situations. Yet when we terminate successful helping relationships without encouraging clients to examine and explore their own potential for caring, our task seems incomplete at best. Egan (1994) suggested finding "ways to get reluctant and resistant clients into situations where they are helping others" (p. 153). Again, however, remember that such encouragement must be tempered by the ethical guidelines of each helper's specialty.

People in the United States have persistently searched for ways to help themselves and others become motivated. Self-motivation is necessary to achieve educational goals, find a successful career path, establish beneficial relationships, and so on. As we have noted throughout this book, it is also requisite for caring relationships. Therefore, reliable assessment of our clients' willingness to help others seems a reasonable step to take in the helping relationship. Just as we monitor our own self-interests and other factors that might be detrimental to our caring relationships, we have a responsibility to measure our clients' capacity to care genuinely for others, particularly if we are encouraging them to become active helpers and caregivers.

We also ensure that students, clients, and patients have support systems in place to assist them when their volunteer caring relationships become especially stressful. It is unrealistic, and sometimes unethical, to expect people with newly learned skills to cope with their own pressing concerns while flourishing in relationships that tax their emotional strength. For example, a widow who has successfully processed her grief through brief therapy might need occasional sessions with a counselor or a support group as she volunteers to help friends, relatives, and others who also have lost a loved one.

When we encourage clients to extend themselves by serving the community, we remember that helping does not end when we accomplish an initial set of goals. In many settings and fields of practice, we have countless opportunities to encourage our clients to extend their caring relationships. When we facilitate such relationships, we broaden our influence and our work as helpers. The opportunities we miss to encourage clients to move to another level of caring neglects their potential to contribute to the community. More important, it ignores the ultimate measure of a healthy functioning person: to express genuine interest in the welfare of other people because *they* want to.

In Chapter 5, we considered four quadrants for caring about others and ourselves both personally and professionally. An essential aspect of helping clients express active concern and interest in the welfare of others is, in a sense, an application of this model. We want to help people move from a level of self-monitoring and self-caring to a level that enables them to care for and about others. To do so, they use skills similar to the self-help strategies they have learned in their own therapeutic sessions and translate those behaviors into helping other people. This process does not begin at the end of our helping relationships. Rather, it is introduced as a long-term objective for each client to consider as she or he sets goals within the relationship.

Starting Early

We can introduce this philosophy early in most of our helping relationships. For example, a child therapist who is helping a young boy learn relaxation techniques to calm himself down during frustrating situations might ask him if these skills could be useful to other family members. Perhaps the boy could share what he has learned in therapy with his parents and siblings.

When possible, we can assess a client's receptivity for caring about others early in the helping relationship. This preliminary assessment may indicate the client's willingness to reach out to others. As noted, this level of "desiring" is the first stage of creating beneficial relationships. The following questions and statements might help us perform a basic assessment in the beginning stages of the helping relationship. This assessment process is not crammed into a single session with the client. Rather, it is meshed with the skills and knowledge we use to help people focus on their identified concerns and problems.

1. *Expression of concern for others.* A primary goal of helping is to have clients focus on their immediate needs. This is why they come to us for assistance. However, it is equally important to encourage them to cultivate concern and interest in other

Reflection

Consider the population with whom you are working or will work with in the future. What opportunities are available to encourage them to help others? If you are realistic about this potential, you will be better able to create usable ideas and practical strategies.

people. We look for ways in which our clients express a willingness to be engaged and involved in the problems of other people. For example, clients who talk about helping people who have suffered from a recent hurricane or other disaster verbalize this desire differently from clients who simply express regret that people have suffered losses. Tuning in to these different expressions enables us as helpers to identify a level of willingness that is imperative for anyone to reach out and help others.

2. *Capacity to listen with empathy.* The measure of effective helping is the degree to which people sense that they are understood and helpers empathize with them. As we work with clients, we can assess their capacity to listen with empathy as well. For example, consider a child counselor who illustrates understanding of a situation by reading a short story that parallels the difficult time the client is expressing. At the same time, the counselor listens to see if the child expresses compassion for the main characters in the story. In group counseling, a counselor assesses how different members exhibit their concern for other participants. The way in which clients respond to stories of people with difficulties or to other group members who share problems is a sign of their capacity to care.

Barriers to effective listening and empathic responding can sometimes be readily identified. Getting ready to talk, mentally arguing instead of listening, avoiding eye contact, and responding with self experiences that downplay the significance of what has been said are a few common examples of reactions from people who demonstrate ineffective listening skills. Identifying these behaviors and traits as deterrents to establishing caring relationships might be helpful to clients and may become part of their therapeutic goals.

3. *Recognition that their problems are not unique.* We can measure our clients' capacity to care by assessing their recognition that other people have similar concerns. This is a particularly important aspect of group work because it creates support for each member by linking common aspects of their problems. By seeing these common elements, clients are more likely to share their experiences with the hope that they can support others as we have supported them in the helping relationship.

4. *Successful past experiences with helping others.* Clients who have experience in reaching out and helping other people are usually in a stronger position to repeat the process. Occasionally, their attempts at helping might be rejected, and they might need our encouragement to start again. More likely, however, we will be able to draw on their successful experiences as indication that they have the ability to help themselves.

Reflection

You might be familiar with barriers to effective listening. If you notice a client demonstrate one of these traits, how can you facilitate better listening? What can you do within an ethical helping relationship?

5. *Ability to express inner satisfaction.* Sometimes our clients are active in the lives of other people, trying to help and please family, friends, and colleagues. In many instances, they enter these relationships to validate themselves and give their own lives greater significance. When encouraging clients to reach out to others, we assess their ability to express inner satisfaction regardless of how much external reward and validation they receive. People who demonstrate a capacity to care only when there is obvious self-benefit probably are not the strongest candidates to become effective helpers. In contrast, people who extend themselves to others simply because they want to and feel more complete as human beings by doing so are in a stronger position to provide genuine care.

6. *Expression of respect and regard for people who are different.* In our helping relationships, we observe countless verbal and nonverbal behaviors, some of which tell us how clients feel about people who are different. Observing our clients' attitudes and reactions to people of diverse religions, races, cultures, physical and mental abilities, or other traits can help us determine their capacity to help people who are different from themselves.

Providing Support

Few helpers are able to provide consistent and dependable service without support systems and resources, regardless of the setting in which they work. By encouraging students, clients, and patients to reach out in helpful ways to others, we commit ourselves to providing the necessary support systems for success. This could mean being available as mentors; providing resources such as manuals and appropriate literature; or referring clients to community agencies, churches, synagogues, recreational facilities, and other institutions that might benefit from their presence as volunteers while providing appropriate support.

We must also ensure that clients' attempts at helping others are balanced with care for themselves. Many people who seek assistance do so because they have lost focus on their own needs. When we show them the importance of maintaining balance in the help they give others with the help they give themselves, we create an internal support system for them.

By assessing our clients' experiences and traits, we are in position to encourage them, during and after the helping relationship, to use their abilities and compassion to reach out to others. At the same time, by providing support for their efforts to

Reflection

Can you remember a time when you hesitated to help someone because he or she was different? Is there anything you would change about the way in which you handled this experience?

care for others, we validate our commitment to them. In this process, voluntary care is extended to many other people through their work and deeds.

FOSTERING INSTITUTIONAL RESPONSIBILITY FOR CARING

As helpers, each of us performs services within the framework of some organization, agency, or institution. Nurses work in hospitals, medical clinics, and nursing homes. Counselors provide services in schools, colleges, mental health centers, family clinics, career placement centers, and other agencies. Social workers and psychologists serve clients in a wide range of governmental, medical, social, and privately operated agencies. Although some of us work in private practice, such settings also create an organizational or institutional climate, which, like the countless human relationships we form, can demonstrate either caring or uncaring attitudes.

Within all of these settings, the sum of our behaviors helps to define a climate of caring. As noted throughout this book, students, clients, and patients ultimately make this determination through their perceptions of the institution or organization. The question for us is, what can we do beyond our individual and small-group helping relationships to ensure that the organizations and agencies we represent consistently demonstrate helpful and beneficial behaviors toward the people we aim to serve? In Chapter 1, we introduced the Five P's model that William Purkey and his colleagues developed to help schools and other organizations assess their overall climate (Purkey & Novak, 1996; Purkey & Schmidt, 1996). A former graduate student, Cris Cannon, and I proposed that the model might also be useful in individual and group helping relationships, such as family counseling (Cannon & Schmidt, 1999). Here, we return to this model as a way to assess the degree to which our agencies and organizations create caring and beneficial climates for the people they serve. Interested readers can find a more in-depth explanation of the Five P's in other sources (e.g., Purkey & Schmidt, 1996; Purkey & Novak, 1996). For our purposes, however, let's consider how *people, places, policies, procedures, and programs* provide a structure for examining the overall soundness and well-being of our organizations.

Purkey and Schmidt (1996) have suggested a relay activity that staff members can use to examine, reflect on, and design proactive strategies to improve an organization's services for customers. Around five tables (one for each "P"), groups of staff members use a combination of brainstorming activities to create lists of concerns, challenges, and solutions that focus on each of the categories. As each small group moves from table to table, a clearer, more specific picture of the situation begins to emerge.

Another activity involves constructing a checklist survey about the organization for staff members and customers to complete. The survey results may be helpful in setting a direction to alter institutional policies, change procedures, or renovate places to facilitate care. Figure 6.1 illustrates a client questionnaire that an institution might use to assess its physical environment and interactions with staff members. This sample can be used as a model for designing questionnaires that assess other aspects (i.e., policies and procedures) of agencies and institutions.

Directions: Use this questionnaire to observe your physical environment and the people in it. Complete the questions based on your observations. Circle the responses that most accurately describe your observations. (Circle *Y* for yes, *N* for no and *UN* for undecided.)

1.	Is the entrance pleasing to the eye, clean, orderly, and in good repair?	Y	N	UN
2.	When you walk in the front door, do you feel welcomed?	Y	N	UN
3.	Is it easy to find your way around the building, and are signs posted to help visitors?	Y	N	UN
4.	Are the inside and outside pleasing to the eye, with attractive colors, artwork, living plants, and furnishings?	Y	N	UN
5.	Are appliances and fixtures such as water fountains, lights, computers, door-knobs, and others in working order?	Y	N	UN
6.	Is the lighting appropriate throughout the building and in parking areas?	Y	N	UN
7.	Is the temperature in the building comfortable?	Y	N	UN
8.	Are restrooms clean and supplied with paper towels, tissues, and soap in the dispensers?	Y	N	UN
9.	Are the outside grounds in good repair—grass mowed, bushes trimmed, equipment safe, and building painted?	Y	N	UN
10.	Are the handicapped accesses well maintained?	Y	N	UN
11.	Is there adequate parking for staff members and visitors?	Y	N	UN
12.	Are safety procedures in place, and are they followed equitably?	Y	N	UN
13.	Does the staff appear friendly to each other and to visitors?	Y	N	UN
14.	Is the agency's telephone answered courteously and helpfully?	Y	N	UN
15.	When services are requested, are they received in a timely manner?	Y	N	UN
16.	Do staff members seem pleased with their employment?	Y	N	UN
17.	Is the staff knowledgeable about the organization and its programs, services, and procedures?	Y	N	UN
18.	Do staff members seek out visitors to offer their assistance?	Y	N	UN

FIGURE 6.1 *Climate questionnaire*

Rojewski and Wendel (1990) suggested several steps to individualize the process of surveying the work climate. Although they specifically focused on measuring school climate, the process also applies to other settings. Their steps to creating an individualized survey include planning, reviewing the literature, developing and organizing themes, developing survey items, administering the survey, analyzing the results, and disseminating and using the results. They compared standardized surveys with an individualized approach, noting that standardized instruments measure common elements and have value depending on their degree of validity and reliability. One drawback of standardized measures, however, is that they may not focus on particular needs and concerns of the organization being surveyed. Thus, it seems appropriate to balance our use of standardized instruments with individualized surveys in order to paint an accurate picture of the caring environment.

The ultimate goal in applying any assessment process or using any structure to examine the organizations in which we serve is to move beyond our individual caring relationships and create systems that adhere to the traits and characteristics espoused in this book. Research, particularly studies of educational organizations, overwhelmingly indicates that the climate we foster in our organizations has a significant impact on achieving our mission. To accomplish this goal, we should measure not only client satisfaction but also employee and volunteer contentment. Many large corporations have discovered that regular surveys of their employees help identify areas of concern; and by addressing these issues, companies encourage their workers to feel that they are a productive and valuable part of the corporate environment.

Caudron (1997) has noted that corporate turmoil has precipitated many employees to reassess the value of their work. As a result, a large number of workers have come to view work and living as two separate goals. Organizations and institutions that care about their employees might want to assess the degree to which people find meaning in their work, are passionate about what they do, and feel valued by the companies that employ them. Nationwide surveys of workers have found that organizations providing identification, appreciation, and appropriate performance measures report higher levels of job satisfaction. At the same time, studies have shown a strong correlation between employees' satisfaction and increased organizational profits.

There are countless ways in which we as helpers can assist our organizations in assessing customer satisfaction; measuring the work environment; and altering places, policies, programs, and processes to create greater care for people. If we truly care, then we will extend this capacity for caring to the larger arena so that we affect more people.

EXPANDING LOVING RELATIONSHIPS

As I was preparing to write this final section of the book, my wife and I became grandparents for the first time. The birth came suddenly, accompanied by some trepidation, when our daughter's physician ordered her to the hospital for an emergency Caesarean section. The evening phone call announcing the impending surgery was

Reflection

Consider the organization in which you spend most of your working hours. Think about the degree of caring it conveys overtly and covertly. What are some areas you would change?

alarming, and we were both filled with anxiety as we began a three-hour drive to the hospital. We arrived to find that the surgery had been successful, our daughter was doing well, and we had a beautiful baby granddaughter.

Reflecting on that evening, with my initial anxiety replaced by wondrous joy, I appreciated the love of my family and the power that love possesses to bring people together to face difficult challenges or celebrate grand events. How fortunate people are when they have loving family members, dear friends, and others in their lives who can extend genuine concern and compassion in times of need and great joy. I also wondered, as a professional helper, if I was doing enough to help my clients move beyond the helping process to establish loving relationships in their lives. We know that fulfilled lives include a variety of relationships and that the ultimate relationship is one of unconditional love. In *A Way of Being*, Carl Rogers (1980) wrote, "I feel enriched when I can truly prize or care for or love another person and when I can let that feeling flow out to that person" (p. 20). This might be an appropriate goal for all students, clients, and patients to set as they move with us beyond individual helping relationships.

Patterson and Hidore (1997) emphasized that all the facilitative conditions orchestrated in therapeutic relationships constitute love in the supreme sense. According to therapist and theologian Thomas Moore, "love is the essence of psychotherapy" (Patterson & Hidore, 1997, p. 91). If we accept this premise, it follows that a beneficial therapeutic relationship can encourage clients to model the love they have received by extending themselves in loving ways to others. Indeed, this step is an essential part of the self-actualizing process for many of our clients. They have experienced success in the helping relationship and now can move that experience toward becoming more fulfilled human beings.

The expansion of love relationships begins with us. All the theorists and philosophers seem to say that our own capacity to love another is intrinsic to our ability to help people with genuine care. How we actively demonstrate our love on a daily basis is a measure of how successful we might be in our professional helping relationships. Love is not a passive process; it is a particularly active one. From the smallest sign of regard we might show a stranger who passes on the street by smiling, nodding, or saying, "Good morning!" to the most demonstrative act of passion and affection we show our dearest loved ones, our loving relationships are an outward expression of the ingredients we believe to be essential in helping relationships. The sum of all these ingredients is the ultimate care we demonstrate for others and ourselves. As with love, the process of caring is an active one; it is the sum total of what we do on behalf of those whom we intend to help.

Reflection

Think about different forms of loving relationships. What qualities and characteristics identify and distinguish these interactions?

While visiting my granddaughter after her birth, I was reading Canfield and Hansen's *A 5th Portion of Chicken Soup for the Soul* (1998) from their popular series. The beginning chapter of this volume is titled "On Love." Reading the chapter's heartwarming and sometimes poignant stories, I began to identify common behaviors and characteristics of the people in these episodes. All of them add to the validity of caring qualities that are fundamental to all helping relationships. They are qualities we want to attain and retain as professional helpers and encourage students, clients, and patients to embrace as well.

Here, we consider 10 conditions necessary for giving ourselves in loving ways to others. They share many similarities with the elements of caring we have examined throughout this book. Combined, these traits, characteristics, and behaviors allow us to become more fulfilled helpers and develop a philosophy to pass along to our clients. In this way, we are able to extend our care beyond the numerous individual helping relationships that we establish throughout our careers.

Seeing Beyond the Apparent

Helpers who illustrate great compassion and love for others begin from a nonjudgmental posture. They look beyond the current, obvious conditions of a given situation and appraise the potential of what might be. This is not an easy task, particularly in a culture that is highly conditioned by appearances, style, and ephemeral trends. In our technologically advanced society, tempting video images and tantalizing sound bites influence us in ways that make it easy to ignore the substance of a person or the significance of an event. In contrast, we strengthen our effectiveness as helpers when we look for the depth and worth of all individuals who seek our assistance.

To be able to demonstrate compassionate love, we must first examine our capacity to care with genuine regard and acceptance, a condition we explored previously in this book. In this self-assessment, we ask ourselves pointed questions about how we receive and accept others. How do we relate to people from different cultures? What reactions do we have when meeting people who are physically challenged or have other conditions that make their appearance different from our own? What beliefs govern our behaviors when helping clients who have intellectual deficiencies or learning problems? How do we relate to people whose cultural norms differ from ours or whose moral values and social standards conflict with ours? Our answers will help us determine whether we have the inner substance to create a solid foundation on which to build truly helpful and loving relationships.

Expecting No Reciprocity

Genuine love exists without the anticipation or contemplation that we will receive something in return. As helpers, we establish our most effective relationships when we suppress our own expectations and defer to the hopes and desires of students, clients, and patients. This does not mean we lack hope or optimism about what might be accomplished through the process of helping. On the contrary, we express confidence in our clients' potential while withholding any expectation of gaining self-worth as a result of facilitating a successful helping relationship.

Likewise, when encouraging clients to seek loving relationships, we may find it useful to teach them about the value of doing good simply for the purpose of being helpful to others. While this is especially true when working with young children, it is also helpful with older clients. The goal is to help all clients move from narcissism to benevolence in their daily relationships. Several practical strategies can be used to help these clients, such as having them care for living plants; forming relationships with pets; or visiting residential care facilities and providing entertainment, companionship, or other assistance to children, adolescents, or older residents. Whatever the strategy, the key ingredient for all of us is to reach out in helpful ways to people, with the only expectation being that we will feel positive about our contribution to their lives.

Being With versus Doing To

There has always been a propensity in American culture to fix things that are problematic, and this philosophy sometimes infiltrates professional and volunteer helping relationships in our society. For example, classroom teachers often want school counselors to change student behavior. Similarly, parents sometimes expect child psychologists to make their children learn better. Married couples want family therapists to suggest ways that their partners might change to make the marriage more fulfilling, and patients want physicians to give them medication or do something that will make them healthier. Although all these relationships depict an active helper's stance, they also advocate a "doing to" posture as opposed to a "being with" relationship. As noted in Chapter 2, a truly caring relationship embraces a "being with" philosophy. Genuine loving relationships exist and thrive according to the same premise.

When loving another person, we avoid manipulative behaviors that denote an element of nonacceptance. We demonstrate our love by being available, supportive, and nurturing at all times and in all circumstances regardless of how trying or difficult the times might be. In truly loving relationships, we are satisfied with being with people because we enjoy their company, value their presence in our lives, and feel complete when we are with them. In such relationships, we exist for and with each other—not to effect change in the other person, but to grow together while becoming more tomorrow than we are today.

Reflection

Revisit a time when you helped someone. Can you remember what, if anything, you gained from this experience?

Participating Actively

Loving relationships are active alliances. Therefore, when we express love to another, we say it with more than words. Telling people how much we love them and how important they are to us is an essential aspect of loving relationships, but we also need to demonstrate this belief on a daily basis. The things we do on behalf of the people we love add credibility to the words we use to express our admiration and affection. By actively showing people, even in quiet and unassuming ways, the depth of our love, we reach for a level of genuineness and authenticity that allows us to be a significant figure in the lives of people for whom we care deeply.

Helping our clients to adopt a posture of participating actively in their love relationships is another way that we expand our influence beyond individual helping relationships. Students, clients, and patients learn that the richness of their own experiences is greatly enhanced when they move beyond personal feelings and desires and take an active role in creating intimate, caring relationships. In helping people take a proactive stance in their love relationships, we model such behavior by actively demonstrating our high regard and concern for their welfare within the helping relationship.

Being Gently Persistent

As we have indicated, some helping relationships can be difficult to establish, and others can be hard to move in a positive direction. This can also be true in our love relationships. Sometimes the people for whom we care the most seem to reject our attempts at helping them. In these instances, we show our resolve by being gently persistent and not giving up on them. By being persistent, we maintain faith in our conviction that the people we care about most have value, even when their behaviors might contradict this belief. At the same time, we demonstrate confidence in ourselves by not taking personally their rejection of our attempts to help.

Both of these qualities can also be valuable to our clients. By learning to be more persistent in their own relationships with others and not taking rejection personally, clients are able to establish a stronger foundation for their own psychological health.

Enjoying Simple Things

One intriguing aspect of loving relationships is their universal enjoyment of simple pleasures. Truly loving relationships do not depend on lavish gifts, extravagant events, or memorable experiences. Although such ingredients might excite any relationship, our most significant loving relationships survive and flourish because we find enjoyment in less noticeable circumstances and experiences.

In our development as helpers, we may also find it useful to enjoy the simpler yet more precious moments with the people we love. Quiet times together, pleasant walks in the park or on the beach, a board game, popcorn and a movie, and a favorite recording are among the limitless experiences that enrich our love relation-

Reflection

What have been the most enjoyable and loving experiences you can recall? How have they enriched your life?

ships. These types of activities exemplify the "being with" philosophy of caring that contrasts with "doing to" or "doing for" mentalities.

Once we are able to enjoy fully the pleasures of all our love relationships, we are in a better position to encourage our clients and patients to do the same. By modeling loving qualities and demonstrating how to elevate personal relationships through the enjoyment of simple pleasures, we offer clients an avenue by which they, too, can establish genuine loving relationships. Many people who seek our assistance do so because they believe their life is insignificant. They are looking for some fantastic yet elusive ingredient to add to their lives and make them happier. For such clients, it might be helpful to teach them the value of an abundance of simple pleasures as opposed to a few memorable moments.

Having Faith

All loving relationships are founded on the belief that mutual caring is beneficial to our well-being and important to a fulfilled life. We frequently enter these relationships when we notice that other people care about us. In return, we demonstrate good faith by reciprocating their attention, concern, and helpfulness. This stance is instrumental in our willingness to enter into professional helping relationships. Clients come to us because they have faith in our ability to help them. In some instances they may be wondering how to choose a direction in life; in others they may be searching for someone to help them solve a difficult problem. We return their confidence by expressing trust in their capability to make decisions that will benefit them and the people they love.

Throughout this book we have emphasized the importance of optimism, trust, perseverance, and related qualities that contribute to our faith in ourselves and others. When we encourage these ingredients with clients, we empower them to reach out to other people, unselfishly and without reward. Encouraging them to increase faith in their fellow human beings is an invaluable strategy that will help them move toward faith in themselves, a requisite for personal growth and development.

Giving

Another common ingredient in loving relationships is the notion of human or spiritual giving. Loving relationships are marked by the devotion of time, the investment of energy, and the development of mutual affirmation that each partner lends to an alliance. This is what we offer when we "give of ourselves" to help other people.

Many people who seek assistance from counselors, therapists, and other helpers would benefit from finding ways to give something of themselves back to their family, community, school, or other group. Sometimes clients are struggling because of perceptions they have of not being treated kindly by others or not having things that others have. As part of our effort to assist these people, we can model the notion of giving by being available to them, facilitating institutional changes that will make their lives less stressful, and finding resources to support their decisions.

Demonstrating Unconditional Love

Because we establish loving relationships without expectation of reciprocation or reward, we also enter them without condition. This is a complex concept to understand, particularly in modern culture, where we are raised from infancy to count on being rewarded for our effort. According to Leo Buscaglia (1972), "the perfect love would be one that gives all and expects nothing. . . . It is only when love demands that it brings on pain" (p. 97). Yet we want all our clients to have safe, loving relationships, and the issue of safety is a paramount expectation. Helping clients understand and accept the concept of unconditional love, while encouraging them to establish healthy and safe relationships, is often the greatest challenge we face as helping professionals.

In helping relationships, we establish what are sometimes referred to as "therapeutic conditions"—those ingredients we use in the helping process to ensure the safety of clients, provide appropriate responses to their concerns and statements, and show unwavering respect for the integrity of the helping relationship. As we have learned throughout this book, these conditions are fundamental to caring. Because therapeutic conditions depend on people's perspectives and statements, "the level of the conditions varies during therapy and in relationship to the behavior of the client" (Patterson & Hidore, 1997, p. 93).

Students, clients, and patients can learn these same conditions to establish healthy, loving relationships in their own lives. Unconditional love does not mean blind love, nor does it mean that we give of ourselves in destructive or unhealthy ways to continue in relationships that are not beneficial to our development. Just as it is essential to demonstrate unconditional love with our clients, it is equally important that we encourage them to extend love to others in positive and enriching ways.

Expressing Intentional Love

All the behaviors and characteristics described here contribute to the intentionality of our loving relationships. In this book, we have examined how our intentionality interacts with our ability to care with utmost regard for people. It follows, therefore, that human intentionality, the inner guidance system that defines our helping relationships, also influences our loving relationships. By monitoring our intentionality and understanding the purpose and direction we give to our loving relationships, we are able to reach higher levels of personal intimacy and satisfaction in our lives. We have greater appreciation of our ability to have faith in others, enjoy simple pleasures of life, appreciate the company of others, actively participate in another's development, and incorporate many other characteristics that contribute to loving relationships.

A television news documentary once examined the plight of children without families, whom the system had labeled "unadoptable." In this broadcast, the reporter told of two children, a brother and sister, who had been moved from foster home to foster home and then to a residential treatment center because they could not be placed for adoption. Of course, both children had many challenges, behaviorally and emotionally. The report continued to reveal how one family became aware of the children's situation and took them into their home. Over time and by overcoming many obstacles, the family's intention began to show evidence of change. Both children came to feel loved as an integral part of the group and were eventually adopted into this family. The family's intentional love not only helped the children adjust their perceptions and behaviors but enabled them to thrive as autonomous persons, no longer categorized by a bureaucracy whose intentionality was not meeting their needs.

In this chapter, we examined several qualities and characteristics that allow us to move our intentional helping and caring for others beyond individual relationships. We do this first by cultivating care with our clients, encouraging them to reach out in helpful ways toward others. Next, we use our knowledge and skill to assess organizations and institutions and seek ways to make them people-oriented in how they do business. Lastly, we value many different types of loving relationships. This chapter has summarized all the beliefs put forth in this book by revisiting the notion that truly caring relationships are those in which unconditional love is demonstrated and experienced. This philosophy and commitment enable us to care in genuine and intimate ways for all the people who seek our assistance. Most of all, the consistent demonstration of these qualities defines us as intentionally caring professionals.

References

Aspy, D., Roebuck, F. N., & Aspy, C. (1983). Physical fitness in counseling and teaching. *Journal of Humanistic Education and Development, 21,* 115–123.

Bandura, A. (1994). Self-efficacy. In V. S. Ramachaudram (Ed.), *Encyclopedia of human behavior* (Vol. 4, pp. 71–81). New York: Academic Press.

Beck, A. T. (1996). Beyond belief: A theory of modes, personality, and psychopathology. In P. M. Salkovskis (Ed.), *Frontiers of cognitive therapy* (pp. 1–25). New York: Guilford.

Berk, L. (1989). Neuroendocrine and stress hormone changes during mirthful laughter. *American Journal of Medical Sciences, 298,* 390–396.

Beutler, L. E., Machado, P. P. P., and Neufeldt, S. A. (1994). Therapist variables. In A. E. Bergin & S. L. Garfield (Eds.), *Handbook of psychotherapy and behavior change* (4th ed., pp. 229–269). New York: Wiley.

Brammer, L. M. (1993). *The helping relationship: Process and skills* (5th ed.). Boston: Allyn & Bacon.

Bugental, J. F. (1980). The far side of despair. *Journal of Humanistic Psychology, 20*(1), 49–68.

Buscaglia, L. (1972). *Love.* New York: Fawcett Crest.

Canfield, J., & Hansen, M. V. (1998). *A 5th portion of chicken soup for the soul.* Deerfield Beach, FL: Health Communications.

Cannon, W. C., & Schmidt, J. J. (1999). Invitational counseling: A fresh vernacular for marriage and family therapy. *Journal of Invitational Theory and Practice, 6,* 73–84.

Caudron, S. (1997). The search for meaning at work. *Training and Development, 51*(9), 24–27.

Clark, D. A., & Steer, R. A. (1996). Empirical status of the cognitive model of anxiety and depression. In P. M. Salkovskis (Ed.), *Frontiers of cognitive therapy* (pp. 75–96). New York: Guilford.

Collingwood, T. R. (1976). Physical functioning: A precondition for the helping process. *Counselor Education and Supervision, 15,* 211–215.

Combs, A. W. (1989). *A theory of therapy: Guidelines for counseling practice.* Newbury Park, CA: Sage.

Combs, A. W., & Gonzalez, D. M. (1994). *Helping relationships: Basic concepts for the helping professions.* Boston: Allyn & Bacon.

Cousins, N. (1979). *Anatomy of an illness.* New York: Norton.

Dass, R., & Gorman, P. (1985). *How can I help?* New York: Knopf.

Egan, G. (1994). *The skilled helper* (5th ed.). Pacific Grove, CA: Brooks/Cole.

Frakes, D. L. (1999). Humor in counseling: A review and examination from an invitational perspective. *Journal of Invitational Theory and Practice, 6,* 85–92.

Fromm, E. (1970). *The art of loving.* New York: Bantam.

Gladding, S. T. (1996). *Counseling: A comprehensive profession* (3rd ed.). Upper Saddle River, NJ: Merrill/Prentice Hall.

Gladding, S. T. (1999). *Group work: A counseling specialty* (3rd ed.). Upper Saddle River, NJ: Merrill/Prentice Hall.

Glasser, W. (1965). *Reality therapy: A new approach to psychiatry.* New York: Harper & Row.

Goodheart, A. (1994). *Laughter therapy.* Santa Barbara, CA: Stress Less.

Hamachek, D. (1992). *Encounters with the self.* New York: Harcourt Brace Jovanovich.

Hamer, R. J. (1995). Counselor intentions: A critical review of the literature. *Journal of Counseling and Development, 73,* 259–270.

Hilyer, J. C., Jenkins, C. W., Deaton, W. L., Dillon, C., Meadows, M. E., & Wilson, G. D. (1980). Physical dimensions of counseling: Perspective for the helping professions. *Counselor Education and Supervision, 20,* 101–116.

Hinkle, J. S. (1988). Psychological benefits of aerobic running: Implications for mental health counselors. *Journal of Mental Health Counseling, 10,* 245–253.

Ivey, A. E., & Ivey, M. B. (1998). *Intentional interviewing and counseling: Facilitating client development in a multicultural society* (4th ed.). Pacific Grove, CA: Brooks/Cole.

Jourard, S. M. (1964). *The transparent self: Self-disclosure and well-being.* Princeton, NJ: Van Nostrand Reinhold.

Kohn, A. (1991). Caring kids: The role of the school. *Phi Delta Kappan, 72*(7), 496–506.

Kottler, J. A. (1992). *Compassionate therapy: Working with difficult clients.* San Francisco: Jossey-Bass.

Kottler, J. A. (1997). *Succeeding with difficult students.* Thousand Oaks, CA: Corwin.

Lefcourt, H., & Martin, R. (1986). *Humor and life stress.* New York: Springer-Verlag.

Magid, K., & McKelvey, C. A. (1989). *High risk: Children without a conscience.* New York: Bantam.

Maslow, A. (1970). *Motivation and personality* (2nd ed.). New York: Harper & Row.

May, R. (1969). *Love and will.* New York: Norton. (Reprinted in 1989 by Doubleday)

Mayeroff, M. (1971). *On caring.* New York: Harper & Row.

McGinn, L. K., & Young, J. E. (1996). Schema-focused therapy. In P. M. Salkovskis (Ed.), *Frontiers of cognitive therapy* (pp. 182–207). New York: Guilford.

Meichenbaum, D. (1985). *Stress inoculation training.* New York: Pergamon.

Meier, S. T., & Davis, S. R. (1993). *The elements of counseling* (2nd ed.). Pacific Grove, CA: Brooks/Cole.

Molm, L. D. (1997). *Coercive power in social exchange.* New York: Cambridge University Press.

Mosak, H., & Maniacci, M. (1993). An "Adlerian" approach to humor and psychotherapy. In W. F. Fry & W. A. Salameh (Eds.), *Advances in humor and psychotherapy* (pp. 1–18). Sarasota, FL: Professional Resource Press.

Noddings, N. (1984). *Caring: A feminine approach to ethics and moral education.* Berkeley: University of California Press.

Noddings, N. (1992). *The challenge to care in schools: An alternative approach to education.* New York: Teachers College Press.

Noel, J. R. (1993). Intentionality in research on teaching. *Educational Theory, 43*(2), 123–145.

Patterson, C. H. (1959). *Counseling and psychotherapy: Theory and practice.* New York: Harper & Row.

Patterson, C. H. (1984). Empathy, warmth, and genuineness in psychotherapy: A review of reviews. *Psychotherapy, 21,* 431–438.

Patterson, C. H., & Hidore, S. (1997). *Successful psychotherapy: A caring, loving relationship.* Northvale, NJ: Aronson.

Purkey, W. W. (1970). *Self-concept and school achievement.* Upper Saddle River, NJ: Prentice Hall.

Purkey, W. W. (1978). *Inviting school success: A self-concept approach to teaching and learning.* Belmont, CA: Wadsworth.

Purkey, W. W. (2000). *What students say to themselves: Internal dialogue and school success.* Thousand Oaks, CA: Corwin.

Purkey, W. W., & Novak, J. M. (1996). *Inviting school success: A self-concept approach to teaching, learning, and democratic practice* (3rd ed.). Belmont, CA: Wadsworth.

Purkey, W. W., & Schmidt, J. J. (1996). *Invitational counseling: A self-concept approach to professional practice.* Pacific Grove, CA: Brooks/Cole.

Rogers, C. R. (1951). *Client-centered therapy: Its current practice, implications, and theory.* Boston: Houghton Mifflin.

Rogers, C. R. (1961). *On becoming a person.* Boston: Houghton Mifflin.

Rogers, C. R. (1980). *A way of being.* Boston: Houghton Mifflin.

Rojewski, J. W., & Wendel, F. C. (1990). Individualizing school-climate surveys. *Clearing House, 63*(5), 202–206.

Ronnestad, M. H., & Skovholt, T. M. (1993). Supervision of beginning and advanced graduate students in counseling and psychotherapy. *Journal of Counseling and Development, 71,* 396–405.

Rutherford, K. (1994). Humor in psychotherapy. *Individual Psychology, 50*(2), 207–222.

Salkovskis, P. M. (Ed.). (1996). *Frontiers of cognitive therapy.* New York: Guilford.

Schmidt, J. J. (1994). *Living intentionally and making life happen* (Rev. ed.). Greenville, NC: Brookcliff.

Schmidt, J. J. (1996). Challenge, confrontation, and exhortation as intentional invitations by professional helpers. *Journal of Invitational Theory and Practice, 4,* 25–36.

Schunk, D., & Zimmerman, B. (1994). (Eds.). *Self-regulation of learning and performance: Issues and educational applications.* Hillsdale, NJ: Erlbaum.

Searle, J. R. (1983). *Intentionality, an essay in the philosophy of mind.* New York: Cambridge University.

Seligman, L., & Gaaserud, L. (1994). Difficult clients: Who are they and how do we help them? *Canadian Journal of Counselling, 28,* 25–42.

Seligman, M. E. P. (1992). *Learned optimism.* New York: Pocket Books.

Sexton, T. L. (1999). Evidenced-based counseling: Implications for counseling practice, preparation, and professionalism. *ERIC Digest.* Greensboro, NC: ERIC Clearinghouse on Counseling and Student Services.

Sexton, T. L., & Whiston, S. C. (1991). A review of the empirical basis for counseling: Implications for practice and training. *Counselor Education and Supervision, 30,* 330–354.

Sweeney, T. J. (1998). *Adlerian counseling: A practitioner's approach.* Philadelphia: Accelerated Development.

Vontress, C. E. (1988). An existential approach to cross-cultural counseling. *Journal of Multicultural Counseling and Development, 16,* 73–83.

Wiggins, J. D., & Weslander, D. (1979). Personality characteristics of counselors rated as effective or ineffective. *Journal of Vocational Behavior, 15,* 175–185.

Williams, A. (1987). Parallel process in a course on counseling supervision. *Counselor Education and Supervision, 26,* 245–254.

Wooten, P. (1992). Laughter as therapy for patient and caregiver. In J. Hodgkin, G. Conners, and C. Bell (Eds.), *Pulmonary rehabilitation* (pp. 422–434). Philadelphia: Lippincott.

Wooten, P. (1994). *Heart, humor and healing.* Mt. Shasta, CA: Communeakey.

Wrenn, C. G. (1973). *The world of the contemporary counselor.* Boston: Houghton Mifflin.

Wrenn, C. G. (1996). *Intelligence, feeling, caring: Some personal perceptions.* Greensboro, NC: ERIC Clearinghouse on Counseling and Student Services.

Wuthnow, R. (1991). *Act of compassion: Caring for others and helping ourselves.* Princeton, NJ: Princeton University Press.

Author Index

Subject Index